Syria 1945–1986

Syria 1945–1986

Politics and Society

DEREK HOPWOOD
St Antony's College, Oxford

London
UNWIN HYMAN
Boston   Sydney   Wellington

© Derek Hopwood, 1988
This book is copyright under the Berne Convention.
No reproduction without permission. All rights reserved.

Published by the Academic Division of
Unwin Hyman Ltd
15/17 Broadwick Street, London W1V 1FP

Allen & Unwin Inc.,
8 Winchester Place, Winchester, Mass. 01890, USA

Allen & Unwin (Australia) Ltd,
8 Napier Street, North Sydney, NSW 2060, Australia

Allen & Unwin (New Zealand) Ltd
in association with the Port Nicholson Press Ltd,
60 Cambridge Terrace, Wellington, New Zealand

First published in 1988

British Library Cataloguing in Publication Data

Hopwood, Derek
  Syria 1945–1986: politics and society.
1. Syria——History——20th century
I. Title
956.91′042   DS98.2
ISBN 0–04–445039–7
ISBN 0–04–445046–X Pbk

Library of Congress Cataloging in Publication Data

Hopwood, Derek.
  Syria 1945–1986: politics and society / Derek Hopwood.
    p.   cm.
  Bibliography: p.
  Includes index.
  ISBN 0–04–445039–7.   ISBN 0–04–445046–X (pbk.)
  1. Syria—Politics and government.   2. Syria—Social conditions.
I. Title.
JQ1825.S8H66   1988
956.91′042—dc19

Typeset in 10 on 12 point Times by Nene Phototypesetters Ltd
and printed in Great Britain by Billing and Sons, London and Worcester

Contents

List of Maps

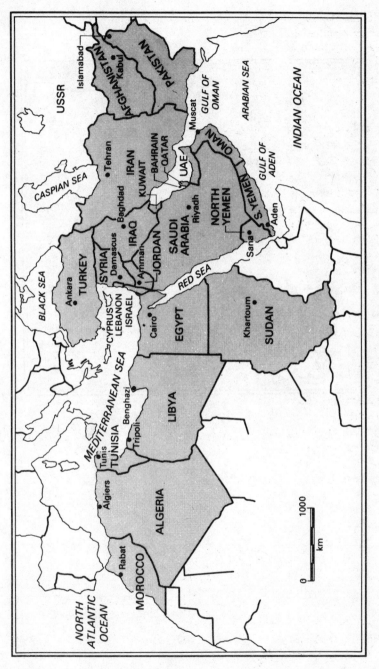

Map 1 Syria's neighbours

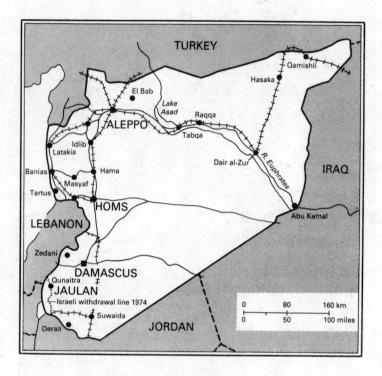

Map 2 Syria

Map 3 Areas occupied by Israel after the 1967 war

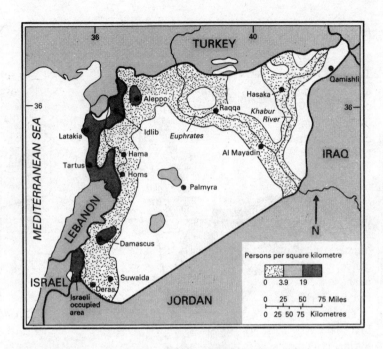

Map 4 Population distribution in the 1970s

Preface

To many outsiders Syria is an enigma. I have written this book in an attempt to understand the country better myself and to pass on my conclusions for the judgement of others. It is only one person's view of the country and there is obviously room for opposing or complementary views. My aim has been to try to explain why Syria behaves as it does and the historical reasons for this behaviour. It has not been written as propaganda or to elicit sympathy. Syria is in many ways a difficult country to write about. Its policy and aims are clear, yet the methods adopted to further them are impossible for many people to accept. The Syrians would assert that they do not act to gain world sympathy. They have certain objectives which they pursue unremittingly. Nevertheless, their external image is of concern to them. If a reader reaches the end of this book he may perhaps be in a better position to make his own judgement on a fascinating country.

This book is based on my interpretation of the works of others, on first hand impressions and on innumerable conversations with Syrian colleagues and friends and with scholars studying Syria. Among them I would like to mention Ruth and Kamal Abu Deeb, great friends and commentators on the Arab and Syrian scenes; Abd al-Nabi Staif, a friend and colleague in Oxford for many years; Salma Mardam, George Jabbur, Philip Khoury, Moshe Maoz and Khairiya Qasimiya, a delightful host in Damascus. Their views, written and spoken, are reflected in these pages as are those of the other scholars whose works I have used. They have helped me to form my own views on Syria which are in the end my responsibility and not theirs. This book, like my earlier one on Egypt, was written for those who may have no previous knowledge of the country or the area. If a specialist reads it he will be annoyed by the statement of the obvious. I have included footnotes to the more important sources. The bibliography includes all those studies I found of help in writing this book. It was completed coincidentally at a particularly difficult period in Anglo-Syrian relations. One can only hope that things will improve.

Derek Hopwood
Oxford, July 1987

1 *Syria and the Syrians*

Our idealism is the optimistic spirit which is confident in itself, its nation and its future. (M. Aflaq)

The Land

Syria is both a country and a concept. The Arabic name for the region in the eastern Mediterranean between Egypt and Turkey is *Sham* which the dictionary defines as 'the northern region, the north, Syria, Damascus'. For the early Arabs looking at the world from their Arabian homeland Sham was a term applied to a largely undefined place across the deserts to their north. They did not use the word *Syria* which was the Greek and Roman name for the province in that area, a name that probably derives from the Babylonian *suri*. To the Arabs it was Sham and usually remained so until the twentieth century when there came into being in a part of that region the modern state of Syria – named thus both by its Arab inhabitants and European statesmen. Sham is still used to signify the whole area – greater Syria – and to underline that, despite political frontiers, there still exists the concept of unity. This greater area is today divided into the states of Jordan, Syria, Lebanon, Israel and the West Bank of the Jordan under Israeli occupation.

It can be roughly defined geographically. In the north stretch the Taurus mountains in Turkey; to the west is the Mediterranean coast; to the east and south are deserts in which man-made boundaries have been drawn and which now march with those of Iraq, Saudi Arabia and Egypt. From north to south the region stretches over 800 kilometres and at its widest is 480 kilometres. The state of Syria comprises over half of the total area. It is triangular in shape with a portion taken out in the south-west where Lebanon is formed. The country is divided into a coastal zone, with a narrow double range of mountains and a large eastern area that includes mountains and vast deserts.

On the Mediterranean there are 160 kilometres of coastline which offer only sheltered coves and no large natural harbour.

Behind the narrow coastal plane the Nusairiya mountain range rises
to 1500 metres and continues down to the Anti Lebanon mountains
where a gap allows access from the coast to the inland city of Homs.
The slopes of the mountains facing the sea benefit from moisture-
laden winds and are more fertile and heavily populated than those
facing the desert which receive only hot dry winds. The mountains
are rather rugged with several deep valleys and ravines and steep
cliffs which are difficult to traverse. On the tops of some of the hills
still stand the imposing ruins of ancient Crusader castles, built to
dominate the coastal plain. The Homs gap provides the only easy
way to the interior from the coast and for centuries has been a
favourite invasion and trade route. Today the railway and road
from Tripoli in Lebanon run through it.

Behind the coastal mountains there is a lower and more extensive
eastern chain which stretches from the Kurdish uplands in the north
to the lofty mount Hermon (2800 metres), one of the most majestic
peaks in Syria, on the border with Lebanon, known in Arabic as
Jabal al-Shaikh – the grey-haired mountain. It drops southward into
the plateaux of the Hauran and the Jaulan Heights.[1] The Hauran,
treeless with few springs but abundant wheat and pasture, rises
again in the east to become the Druze mountain, a high volcanic
region.

Between the two long ranges of mountains lies a rift valley.
Through it runs one of Syria's few rivers, the meandering Orontes,
which rises in Lebanon and reaches the sea near Antioch in Turkey
after a journey of 270 kilometres. On its way it waters the fertile
Ghab region to the north of the Homs gap. Damascus itself is
watered by the Barada river, rising in Lebanon and expiring in the
desert. It has created the Ghuta oasis south of the city which was the
basis of Damascus' prosperity.

Fertile Crescent

The Fertile Crescent is the name given to a large area of cultivable
land stretching from the northern Arabian desert round to the Gulf.
The western section lies in Syria and includes the fringes of the
desert at the foot of the eastern mountain chain, the Hauran,
Damascus oasis, the plains of Homs, Hama and Aleppo, and the
area known as the Jazira (the 'island'), a fertile area in north-
eastern Syria lying between the two rivers, the Tigris and the

Euphrates. It forms part of the larger area now mostly in Iraq, formerly known as Mesopotamia – 'between two rivers' in Greek. The Euphrates with tributaries is the longest and most important river in Syria (670 kilometres) and represents more than 80 per cent of the country's water resources. It rises in Turkey, passes through Syria and flows into the Gulf at Basra.

The rest of Syria is desert, largely uncultivable and home for the Bedouin. It ranges from barren, waterless and stony wastes to areas where shrubs and thistles grow providing scanty grazing for the flocks of nomadic or semi-nomadic tribes. Despite the barrenness, scattered oases and wells make travel across parts of the desert relatively easy.

Climate

The two main influences on the Syrian climate are the sea and the desert. The contrasts between the two influences are modified by the ranges of mountains running parallel to the coast. There are high rainfall and humidity by the sea and high temperatures which reach 30°C in the summer. Heat and humidity can make life unpleasant in the Mediterranean coastal towns. In Lebanon where the mountains rise above Beirut, many city dwellers enjoy the drier, cooler air of mountain villages as a relief from the city. In Syria the mountains are much less accessible to the urban population.

The desert affects inland Syria. Less rain falls – in some areas none at all – and the temperatures rise to the mid-40s. Hot, dust-laden winds blow over the cities and make life difficult when the heat and dust irritate and fray tempers. In the central rift valley a typical 'Syrian' climate prevails – hot, almost cloudless summers and relatively cold winters. The spring, sudden and short, lasts for a few weeks in March and April when even the deserts are covered with flowers and grass. The long hot summers are of the type that prevail throughout the Middle East and to which life styles are adjusted. This is relentless summer; temperatures exceed 35°C in the shade and the glaring light accentuates the shadows. Homes are shuttered, markets covered, and the streets lively with pedestrians in the evening when the daytime heat has slightly subsided. Outdoor cafés are full until late at night and shopkeepers sit gossiping and waiting for custom outside their shops. In November the first heavy showers wash the dust from the leaves; it is autumn.

Water

The Nile is life to Egypt, the Tigris-Euphrates to Iraq. There is no single element in Syria which draws the country together in a similar fashion. Nevertheless, water resources have to be carefully used and economically exploited. Rainfall is badly distributed and varies from year to year. Sixty per cent of the land receives less than 25 centimetres of rain and only 10 per cent has enough rain to maintain regular cultivation. The rivers do not on the whole lend themselves to irrigation. The Euphrates has swift currents and until recently water was only used locally on its banks. The Tabqa Dam now completed has changed this age old picture (see page 108). On the Orontes river huge wooden wheels were used for centuries to raise water for irrigation. They were a Roman invention and, powered by the current of the river, irrigated fields and orchards near Homs and Hama. A guide book of 1875 described them as having 'an odd look, and an odder sound, turning lazily, emptying their shallow buckets, and moaning all the while as if in agony'.[2] They have slowly fallen into disuse, however, their agony silenced as a new dam on the river has lowered the water level and cut off the power to turn them. Modern motor pumps are taking over.

The Barada near Damascus has been extensively used to irrigate the fields and orchards of the city. The water is allocated over the land through an intricate system of channels and dams. Elsewhere in Syria scarce water supplies are carefully preserved and exploited, usually through wells or skilfully built underground irrigation canals.

Towns and Cities

Just as there is no single river uniting Syria, so the towns and cities have served as focuses for regional rather than national loyalty. Damascus, the capital, is one of a number of cities competing for loyalty. Each town (or agro-city – that is, the urban area and its agricultural hinterland from which it draws its food and to which it sells a part at least of its manufactures) has remained important as the framework for social, economic and political participation in society. The weight of local feeling cannot be overstressed in trying to understand the complex of Syrian politics. There are nine such agro-cities, some larger and more important than others. Each includes a city of at least 50,000 people, several towns and perhaps hundreds of villages. In the south is Qunaitra in the Jaulan area, Suwaida in the Druze region, Deraa in the Hauran. These three are smaller than the others but nevertheless stand as centres for a different network of villages. To their north lies Damascus; in the more densely populated north-west are Homs, Hama and on the coast the main port of Latakia. Aleppo in the north is Syria's second city in size and importance to Damascus. Rather remote from other urban areas is Dair al-Zur, far to the east on the river Euphrates, a centre for the fertile lands to the north and the desert area to the south.

Damascus rightly claims to be one of the oldest continuously inhabited cities in the world. Known in the days of Abraham it appears in the Old Testament and was in the eighth century BC a dependency of the Assyrians. Alexander the Great conquered the area in 333 BC, and it remained Greek until 64 BC when Pompey proclaimed Syria a Roman province with Antioch to the north (now in Turkey) as its capital. It was under Roman rule when the apostle Paul experienced his conversion on the road to Damascus. The present day visitor is still shown the house where he is said to have rested and the (far from original) window from which he was let down in a basket. Christianity flourished in the city under the Byzantines until AD 643 when invading Arab armies from central Arabia conquered the city once and for all in the name of Islam.

The Greeks and Romans gave the ancient city its basic street plan which remained the skeleton of the medieval one. Large rectangular walls were built on the bank of the Barada, pierced by seven gates. Remains of these walls and gates can still be seen today. Two long parallel streets crossed the walled enclosure, one forming the basis of the Street called Straight (although it lies buried several feet below the present day thoroughfare). The Muslims built on the existing city, often utilizing existing materials and buildings. The glory of the city was (and is) the Great Mosque of the Umayyads, built on the site of the church of St John the Baptist. Other Muslim buildings gradually changed Damascus from a Graeco-Roman city into an Islamic one, facing towards the desert and the Semitic world. The Mosque was erected as a 'symbol of the political supremacy and moral prestige of Islam'. For a time Damascus was the capital of the whole Islamic world, a period of glory and authority never to be repeated. After AD 750 it became a provincial town when imperial authority passed to Baghdad. Damascus fell under the rule of various foreign and local dynasties, some members of which added to the buildings of the city, but who more often caused damage.

Because of the uncertainty of the times (until the twelfth century) the population began to seek more security and the face of the city changed. Each district barricaded itself behind walls and gates into watertight compartments which were virtually self-sufficient. Christians, Jews and Muslims lived in their separate areas. This development gave the old city its 'Middle Eastern' appearance – small lanes, blind alleys, houses turned in on themselves. When more settled conditions returned, new areas were developed. New religious buildings were put up and the city walls and towers were strengthened or rebuilt. This was during the period of the Crusades although the city itself was not attacked. The Muslim leader Saladin was buried in Damascus to the north of the Great Mosque in a tomb which nearly eight hundred years later assumed a new historical significance.

During this long era the city gradually expanded into the surrounding areas. Each period left its mark in buildings and developments. By the nineteenth century, under the Ottoman Empire European influence was beginning to make itself felt. European consuls, merchants and missionaries took up residence in new houses in the Christian quarter while the old town began to empty and new quarters grew up, particularly on the slopes of the Kasiyun Hill where the Turkish aristocracy built their beautiful houses surrounded by gardens. In 1863 French contractors made a road from Damascus through the mountains to Beirut on the coast to enable travellers to make by stage coach the journey which had previously been on horse or donkey. A railway was added in 1894, also built by a French company. In 1908 a German firm built the famous narrow gauge Hijaz railway from the city to Medina in Arabia to take Muslims on the pilgrimage to Mecca in greater comfort. (This was the railway attacked by the Arabs with Lawrence of Arabia several times during the First World War.)

After 1920 Damascus found itself a colonial city in French hands and as elsewhere the occupiers began to try to impose their own identity on the area. A French town planner and an architect drew up a city development plan which was put into operation in collaboration with the Syrian services. New suburbs, often with tree-lined roads, were developed and, as in other cases, the old city was left almost untouched. Whereas on the whole the French did not live in the old city, Syrians and French mixed in the new areas. Since independence Damascus has continued to expand as the capital of the Syrian Arab Republic, becoming a centre of industry, culture and development and attracting more and more immigrants. In the 1980s its population had reached more than one million.

Aleppo rivals Damascus in antiquity and history and no other place which is still inhabited and flourishing can boast of a comparable history. It dominates its surrounding area and inspires a loyalty which has traditionally been opposed to Damascus. It developed as an important city in the Greek and Roman empires and fell to the Arabs in AD 636. Several dynasties struggled to rule the city and it was at one time (1100) under attack by the Crusaders. Under the descendants of Saladin, Aleppo became one of the most beautiful and active cities in the Middle East. Dominated by its splendid citadel, it was adorned with mosques, markets and schools. From its position on the borders of Anatolia and on the routes to inner Asia, Aleppo became an important trading centre, importing from and exporting to Europe. The Ottomans continued to adorn the city so that today it possesses the most beautiful markets in the Muslim world. European merchants settled there and added to the varied nature of the population.

Under the Ottoman government Aleppo was a province in its own right. Often its links through trade were with Anatolia, the coast and upper Mesopotamia rather than Damascus to the south. It was only after 1918 that Aleppo was incorporated into Syria and developed as the flourishing second city of the republic. This did not mean, however, that it lost its own feeling of separate identity or its independence of thought. The modern city has now spread in an unplanned fashion into the outskirts.

Both Homs and Hama on the road between Damascus and Aleppo are towns dating back to antiquity. Homs is the centre of an intensively cultivated area in the Orontes valley and is now an important city. Hama grew up as a market mainly for the Bedouin from the surrounding districts and has expanded into another modern urban complex. The two towns have been the bases of important families in Syrian politics and therefore are also rivals to Damascus.

Islam

The towns and cities of Syria have tended to underline regional rather than national feelings. Sectarian loyalties also have a tendency to work against national loyalty. Although Syria is overwhelmingly Sunni Muslim, members of the various minority sects have played and continue to play important roles in the country.

The religion of Islam was first proclaimed by the Prophet Muhammad in the early years of the seventh century AD in the towns of Mecca and Medina in present day Saudi Arabia. His message was a simple faith – obedience to God (Allah) and his Prophet, strict observance of the practices and rituals of the community as laid down in God's word – the Quran – and exemplified in the life and acts of Muhammad, which together are called the *sunna* – 'practice' or 'usage'. Muslims who follow this path are consequently named *Sunni* which is usually translated as 'orthodox'. By force of circumstances Muhammad became the leader of the citizens of Medina for whom he had to establish a system of government, of laws and institutions. Islam became a total way of life, regulating public and private activity. For thirteen centuries this religion has been at the root of life and society in Syria. First and foremost Syria is a Muslim country. The Great Mosque in Damascus has been the focus of religious life and learning and is considered to be the fourth holiest place in the Islamic world after Mecca, Medina and Jerusalem. No visitor to Damascus can fail to be struck by the number of mosques, the calls to prayer and the celebration of Muslim festivals, especially during and after the fast of Ramadan. Islam is deeply rooted and is valued (even by Christians) as an essential part of the country's heritage. As in the West, religious festivals may be observed with scant conviction but in Syria Islam is widely and sincerely observed and there are now clear signs of a re-appreciation of Islam as the centre of many people's lives. In Damascus the scholarly tradition has maintained its leading position through the prestige of the Great Mosque. In the poorer quarters of the city, in some provincial towns and villages a less intellectual, more popular form of religion, often connected with local saints, has been prevalent.

Many Syrians would recognize Islam as a bond in their life and as a factor uniting them, although there have been and still are those who question the place of religion in society and have tried to find a means of reconciling religion with the scientific, social and economic ideas of the twentieth century; and there are those who have abandoned the attempt and have turned to secularism. On the other hand, there is very clearly in Syria (and in the Middle East in general) a strong current of religious feeling which preaches that the only hope for society in the contemporary world is a return to the original form of Islam as practised by Muslims at the time of the Prophet.

Muslim Minorities: Shia

The most important schismatic sect in Islam, that named the *shiat Ali* which means 'party of Ali', began as a political movement among the Arabs in the seventh century AD. Ali, the son-in-law of the Prophet Muhammad and fourth caliph (successor to the Prophet) made his base in Iraq. When on his death the political centre of Islam moved to Syria and to a new dynasty, the Arabs of Iraq began an opposition movement in the name of the heirs of Ali. Gradually this political opposition inspired a new doctrine (opposed to the accepted doctrine of the Sunnis) which claimed the exclusive right of Ali's heirs to the caliphate. Feelings were intensified after Ali's two sons, Husain and Hasan, were killed by their opponents. As one Shii historian has written, 'Never has a more disastrous event befallen Islam'. Their martyrdom is still marked annually by mourning ceremonies and plays. The Shia developed a deep attachment to their slain heroes and to their hidden leaders (*imams*) whose reappearance all Shiis await. Their religion is a particularly intense kind of devotion and the supreme reward is martyrdom in battle fighting for their cause. Shiism spread to several parts of the Islamic world and is now the majority religion of Iran. There are also Shiis in Iraq, Yemen and Lebanon.

Shii Sects

Shiism itself has split into a number of more esoteric branches, some of which are represented in Syria. There is a small group of Ismailis, so-called after Ismail, one of their early imams. The ancestors of the Syrian Ismailis were known to Europe as the Assassins, men who were prepared to carry out suicide attacks against the Crusaders. (Their name comes from *Hashishiyin*, takers of *hashish* which supposedly boosted their courage before their attacks.)

More important are the Alawis (followers of Ali) or Nusairis, Syria's largest religious minority. They live chiefly along the coast near Latakia although the town itself is Sunni. Their religion is a mysterious amalgam of pre-Islamic features, extreme Shiism and Christian elements. They deify Ali and are very secretive about their practices, which they refuse to explain to outsiders. They claim they are Muslim but some strict Sunnis do not recognize them as such. Their present importance derives from the fact that the president of Syria, Hafiz al-Asad, and many members of the ruling élite are Alawis.

The Druzes

The Druzes form Syria's third largest religious minority and live largely in the rugged Druze mountain area in the south-west. There are also Druze populations in Lebanon and Israel. They are Muslims, viewed as heretical by Sunnis as they believe one of the caliphs in tenth-century Egypt to have been divine. They have developed their own religion in a closed community which keeps its doctrines secret. They frown on intermarriage and try to forbid both conversion and apostasy. They have tried to govern themselves as far as possible in their mountain retreats and now form a homogenous people with distinctive physical features and social customs, dominated by their own aristocracy and ruling families. They are proud and fiercely independent and make good fighters. Their mountain homes have prevented domination by outsiders.

Christians

Christians form a small yet relatively important community in Syria. The largest group are Arab members of the Orthodox church, the church of Greece and Russia which grew out of the split between Byzantium and Rome. For centuries the Orthodox in Syria were governed by a Greek patriarch resident in Constantinople and an absent Greek hierarchy which neglected the local church. The Arab laity and priests bitterly resented this situation and in the late nineteenth century struggled successfully to elect an Arab patriarch of Damascus. This election was described as the 'first real victory for Arab nationalism'. It was an indication of the Orthodox Arab's devotion to the nationalist cause which has lasted to this day and it raised questions which have been difficult to solve. How can a Christian Arab remain true to his heritage and religion and yet take part with his Muslim Arab brothers in the greater affairs of his country? This problem was made more complex by the uniquely Arab contribution to Islamic civilization. Was it possible to be really Arab without being Muslim?

There could be only one positive response to this dilemma. The Christian Arab had to emphasize what united him with rather than divided him from the other Arabs. This could be done in several ways: by invoking common race, language or nationality, by showing what Islam and Christianity had in common, or by adopting a totally secular approach. The Orthodox Arabs chose on the whole a positive response and joined the Arab nationalist movement. They have been active in political parties and in government and have tried to identify with the majority while still retaining their own identity. The Orthodox are relatively more urbanized than the Muslims and have often been successful businessmen. Proportionately more Christians are educated beyond primary level and more of them are in white-collar and professional occupations.

The Christians benefited from the activities of European missionaries in the nineteenth century who offered a separate educational system. The danger was evident that a Western-type education might alienate them from their Muslim neighbours who attended more traditional schools. The Europeans who brought education did in fact cause disruption to the traditional pattern. They influenced the minds of the children and their parents who began to look to one of the European powers as a protector against possible Muslim intolerance. The Orthodox were 'protected' by Holy Russia until the 1917 Revolution. Soviet Communists were not interested in such activities and left the Orthodox Arabs more or less alone. This was to their benefit and partly for this reason they decided to throw in their lot with the Muslim majority.

The Arab Catholics, Roman and Uniate (those who keep their own liturgy but recognize the authority of Rome, such as the Maronites in Lebanon), have tended to identify more with the West, particularly France. They have thus been more wary of Arab nationalism and have sometimes been accused of preferring the West to the Arab world. The Maronites in Lebanon have carried this to the extreme of fighting their Muslim neighbours in an effort to keep the country Christian and escape Muslim domination. The

2   The Emerging State

We are performing the role of those who prepare.

(M. Aflaq)

History to 1914

Although Syria has an immensely long history stretching back to around 2500 BC, it is not the history of a unified and cohesive state. From 2500 BC to AD 1945 there was hardly a time when Syria as a whole was an independent sovereign state under local rulers. Numerous empires and external powers marched across Syria and incorporated the area into their territory. The Persians, the Pharaohs, the Greeks and Romans came and went. For over 300 years Syria was absorbed into the ancient Egyptian empire. For an even longer period Syria was part of the Graeco-Roman world. Despite these long years of foreign domination something remained recognizably Syrian. There was a local population and culture which did not become Egyptianized or Hellenized. The people did not lose their national character and identify with the Graeco-Roman way of life. Hellenization was skin-deep and only in towns. The population was a mixture of peoples known from Biblical times – Canaanites, Phoenicians, Aramaens and Hebrews, who had evolved their local form of Semitic religion and language (Aramaic).

In addition there were three Arab groups which had founded early Syrian states. They were kingdoms on the desert frontiers and they owed their origins to the settling of nomadic tribes and their participation in trade. They had first appeared in the Arabian desert areas and so can properly be called Arab, although they developed a more cosmopolitan culture. Their most famous cities are the 'rose-red' city of Petra with its splendid monuments carved from the living rock and Palmyra (Tadmor in Arabic) which later became a Roman city. The three kingdoms lasted together from about the sixth century BC until the seventh century AD. They are important for the fact that they were Arab and provided a continuity in time and space for a Syrian Arab culture which came from Arabia, was mediated through them and handed on to the Arab Muslim conquerors of Syria. They are looked upon with pride by contemporary Syrians as proof of an Arab historical identity which existed despite the presence of foreign rulers.

In AD 635 an Arab army fighting under the banner of Islam appeared in the area. This event heralded a profound change in the history of Syria – its permanent integration into the Arab and Islamic worlds. Eventually, Arabic became the language and Islam the religion of most of the population. Syria was no longer part of the Christian Graeco-Roman world and its history became integrated with that of the other Arabs. For a time Damascus was the capital of an Arab empire which stretched from Persia to Spain until the centre of gravity shifted to Bagdad in 750. From then on Syria was either ruled from outside or was split up among a number of smaller dynasties. Major events included the arrival of the Crusaders who occupied only the coastal areas and did not capture any large inland Syrian towns. The Crusader kingdoms of Tripoli, Antioch, and Jerusalem were all outside present day Syria. Most important to Syrian history was the eventual emergence of a local dynasty under the leadership of the famed Saladin, which was able to inflict heavy defeats on the Crusaders and expel them from Jerusalem in 1187. Syrians look upon him as a hero who drove out foreign invaders. If some contemporary attitudes are based on a certain interpretation of history, then it is important to remember the fact of Saladin succeeding, after a long struggle, in expelling the occupier when the Syrian attitude towards the French occupation is later considered. Even attitudes towards Israel are coloured by the belief that in the end the foreign invader is defeated.

Under Saladin Syria and Egypt were united and the capital moved to Cairo. The rulers who followed and who governed Egypt and Syria from 1250 to 1576 were the Mamlukes. They were originally slave soldiers (in Arabic *mamluk* means 'owned') who had been purchased in the slave markets of Russia and the Caucasus as bodyguards for the rulers of Egypt and who eventually seized power themselves. Despite the fact that they were a turbulent lot, often uncultured and bloodthirsty, they were able to clear the area of the last Crusaders and even more importantly to check the advance of the Mongol hordes into western Asia and Egypt. Aleppo, where 50,000 inhabitants were massacred, had fallen. Hama fell and Damascus was threatened. The Mamluke army then rallied and crushed the invaders at a battle near Nazareth in 1260. Under some of the more able Mamluke rulers cultural life flourished and numerous splendid mosques and other buildings were erected. They were in decline towards the end of their rule and were ousted by the rising power in the Middle East – the Ottoman Turks, the invading nomad soldiers from Central Asia who had destroyed the Byzantine Empire.

In 1453 the Ottomans captured Constantinople which became Istanbul and the capital of their expanding empire. In addition to threatening Europe they also turned towards the Arab world. Their powerful army defeated the weakening Mamluke power in 1516 and Syria passed quietly into Ottoman hands where it remained for four centuries. Many other parts of the Arab world were also taken into the Ottoman Empire and, until the end of the First World War, Arab and Turkish history was closely intertwined. Syria was governed in various ways with Damascus as an administration centre. Although fellow Muslims, the Ottomans were not Arabs and remained separate from the local population. Turkish became the language of administration while Arabic remained the language of the Syrian people and of religion. There was no attempt at Turkish colonization and the ethnic and political structure of Syria was not seriously affected by the Ottoman conquest. Turkish governors and soldiers came and went and taxes had to be paid. Syrian society remained Arab and Muslim and while there was a sense of being Ottoman, Syrian allegiance remained with local Arab leading families and officials who were used and trusted as intermediaries with the Ottoman authorities. Some of the families, coming from one of the large towns, gained a prestige which was to last after the Turks had left.

The nineteenth century was the beginning of change in the Middle East. New, sometimes disturbing ideas began to circulate and threatened to disrupt traditional patterns of life – ideas of equality (between Muslims and Christians), modernization, reform and nationalism. Most of these came to the Middle East from Europe and were gradually integrated into local society. Nationalism became a potent force; the other concepts were more difficult to deal with. It was soon realized that European resources and invention were putting the West ahead in industry and technology and these developments influenced thinking in the Middle East as people asked themselves why Christian Europe was making such progress. Did the Muslim world need to accept innovations from the West? In what ways, if any, did it need to reform itself? Could it accept Western ideas and values and still remain true to its Islamic heritage? These and similar questions were put at the time and are still relevant today.

Early signs of change were brought about by Napoleon's invasion of Egypt which he saw as a means of threatening the growing British power in India. In 1798 French troops landed near Alexandria and soon occupied Cairo. They marched on Palestine but were checked by the local ruler with the help of the British fleet at the battle of Acre in May 1799. The French had defeated the Mamlukes who had continued to rule Egypt under the Ottomans. British pressure soon forced the French to leave and in the confused aftermath there arose a new dynasty under a powerful leader, Muhammad Ali. He was of Albanian origin and used the country to further his own ambitions. He was a formidable man who inaugurated a new era in Egyptian history by changing it economically and socially. He welcomed European influence and he sent students to study abroad and invited European training missions to Egypt. He also had wide military ambitions and his armies under his son Ibrahim invaded and occupied Syria during the years 1831–40.

This comparatively short stay brought about fundamental changes. Ibrahim expelled the Ottoman rulers and introduced reforms which were far-reaching and which undermined Syrian traditions. He unified the country under a strong central administration (the first time for centuries), collected taxes and conscripted Syrians into his armies. He created local administrative councils on which Christians and Jews were represented. Large-scale economic and agricultural development was also undertaken and he opened the country to European goods and ideas. Imported cotton and other goods harmed local trade in Damascus and Aleppo and the populations of these two cities had declined by 1840. At the same time European missionaries and consuls began to intervene in local affairs. The missionaries opened schools and colleges which offered Western education to students, primarily Christians, who had little previous knowledge of Europe. The consuls offered 'protection' to different religious groups and in so doing turned their protégés' minds from local concerns to wider horizons. All these moves upset the traditional balance of society especially as it was the Christians who seemed to gain most, achieving equality with the Muslims to whom they previously had had inferior status. The European powers were drawn directly into this situation. France had traditionally claimed an influence in Syrian affairs, a rather bogus claim but one which was to have great significance later. France supported Ibrahim in his policies in Syria, especially those which gave greater freedom and equality to the Christians. Eventually the Muslim population resented these changes and expressed its opposition in a series of uprisings against the Egyptian occupiers. Britain, more than ready to obstruct the French, took the opportunity to support the Ottomans in finally ousting the Egyptians from Syria in 1840.

What had happened during those ten short years? Syria had experienced security and a regular system of government, perhaps also a new sense of political cohesion, and an opening to European activity and influence. It was the beginning of a new era in Syrian history. The Ottomans returned, determined to resume their position of authority and to introduce certain reforms. They were now acting under the close scrutiny of the European powers. The Ottomans disliked this but were by then too weak to offer much resistance. At the same time Egypt was slipping from Ottoman control; Algeria had been occupied by France and taken from the Ottomans. There was greater European economic, educational and political intervention which continued until the outbreak of the First World War. In the latter part of the nineteenth century under the autocratic Ottoman Sultan, Abd al-Hamid, a heavy-handed dictatorship was imposed on the empire which led the Syrians to try to think of ways of improving an oppressive situation.

One obvious answer was national independence – but on what basis? Within the Ottoman Empire? On the territory of Greater Syria? Within a larger Arab entity? The first stirrings of Arab nationalism came from a small group in Beirut in the 1870s which called for the strengthening of feelings of patriotism and love of one's country, in this case Syria. There was as yet little call to break away from the Ottoman Empire, rather to develop Syria within it. Their slogan was 'Our homeland is the Empire, our country Syria'. By 1912 a party had been formed which demanded 'decentralization' in the empire, by which the Arabs would be given much more autonomy with Arabic as their official language. An Arab congress met in Paris in 1913, attended by 25 participants, 23 of them Syrian, which called for greater Arab participation in the affairs of a reformed Ottoman Empire. Other Arabs were convinced, however, that they would never gain equality with the 'imperial' Turks and that they would have to fight for independence. They had begun to think of means of implementing this aim when everything was turned upside down by the outbreak of the First World War.

The First World War

What was said and done during the First World War in relation to the Arab world, particularly Greater Syria, has been the subject of endless controversy. The Ottoman Empire eventually sealed its own fate by deciding to ally itself with Germany and Austria and it faced defeat together with the Central Powers. For Britain and France victory in Europe over the Kaiser's Germany was the all-important goal and most resources were thrown into the battles in the trenches. However, in the Middle East other important fronts were opened. The burden of these was carried by British and Imperial troops. The best known is the defeat of Gallipoli. Other fighting took place in Mesopotamia. In 1917 the Ottomans attacked across the Sinai desert in an attempt to seize the Suez Canal. The British counterattacked and began a campaign that led to the capture of Jerusalem and Damascus and ended with the defeat of the Ottoman army at the battle of Armageddon in September 1918. In these battles there was a feeling of reliving the Crusades and when in December 1917 the British commander, General Allenby, entered Jerusalem humbly on foot it was felt that the Holy City had finally been retaken for Christendom. The Arabs were less sure that they welcomed the replacement of their Ottoman masters by Europeans.

In any case the Arabs had been fighting their own battle. The Arab Revolt began in 1916 under the leadership of Sharif Husain of the Hashimite family. (The Hashimites, descendants of the Prophet Muhammad, had been appointed guardians of the holy cities of Mecca and Medina by the Ottomans and had become virtual rulers of the territory there – the Hijaz.) Husain cherished hopes of widening his rule to include Arabia, Iraq and Syria. He and his sons, Faisal and Abdallah, were ambitious men and the British decided to back them in their ambition to drive the Ottomans from the area. The two sides came to an agreement enshrined in documents called the Husain–McMahon correspondence. (McMahon was British High Commissioner in Egypt.) The Sharif would lead an Arab revolt against the Turks in return for British aid and promises of future independent rule over Arab territories which were rather imprecisely defined. Husain later claimed that he had been promised Iraq, most of Arabia and all of Greater Syria. The British denied that they had ever intended so wide a Hashimite rule as there were competing interests and claims to be taken into account.

It is now no longer clear just what McMahon intended to promise nor exactly what Husain expected. What *is* clear is that after the war Husain and the Arabs expected much more than they got. Had he been given all the territory he claimed, there was no guarantee that all the Arabs would have accepted his rule. He was not Syrian or Iraqi and his family influence had been limited to Hijaz. Among the other interests which the British had to take into account were those of the French. France and Britain were engaged in a life and death struggle against Germany and whatever happened in the Middle East the war in Europe had to take first place. From Britain's point of view the support of the French was essential and they could not be alienated. If Arab demands clashed with those of the French, the French would come first. In March 1915 Britain and France had come together to discuss the future of the Middle East once the Ottoman Empire was defeated.[1] Both countries had firm ideas about their spheres of interest. Thus the Sykes–Picot agreement[2] recognized French pre-eminence in Syria and Lebanon, British in Palestine and Iraq. This arrangement was made without any consultation of those directly concerned, the Arab inhabitants of the area, and would obviously conflict with the promises made to Sharif Husain if the term 'interest' was interpreted as allowing direct interference.

Another piece of European manoeuvring, seen as duplicity by the Arabs, was the issuing by Britain of the Balfour Declaration in 1917. This was in the form of a letter sent by Arthur Balfour, the British Foreign Secretary, to Lord Rothschild, who represented the Zionist organization, stating that Britain viewed with favour the establishment of a national home in Palestine for Jews who wished to emigrate there. Since their expulsion Jews had hoped to return to the land of Israel and its capital Jerusalem. This hope had been expressed in religious terms. In the late nineteenth century it had been transformed into Zionist nationalism, a movement which claimed Palestine as the national homeland of the Jews. Active Zionists gained the support of some British politicians during the First World War and this led to the declaration. To the Arabs at the time, and until today, this document smacked of deceit. The population of Palestine in 1917 was more than 90 per cent Arab,

who were looking forward to the end of Ottoman rule and to
independence. How then could the British government promise to
encourage the large-scale immigration of another people? In
accepting later the Mandate for Palestine Britain undertook to
secure the establishment of the Jewish national home. Arab
opposition was immediately aroused as Palestine was amputated
from Greater Syria and dreams of an independent region were
shattered. This had an incalculable effect on Syrian politics and
history and on Syrian society which from then on was dedicated to
driving the Zionists from Palestine and later to destroying the State
of Israel founded by them on Palestinian territory.

Thus Greater Syria began its 'independent' life at the end of the
First World War in a way very different from that conceived by the
leaders of the Arab revolt. Led by Faisal the Arab army had
harassed the Turkish troops in Arabia in hit-and-run sorties and in
attacks on the Hijaz railway. Among the British officers who helped
with liaison work and advice was T. E. Lawrence, 'Lawrence of
Arabia', who in his own estimation led the revolt and according to
Arab historians played only a minor role. The army moved across
the desert and captured by surprise the port of Aqaba, now in
Jordan. From there they moved into Palestine and Syria and ended
with a dash towards Damascus. The revolt culminated with the
entry of Arab soldiers into the city under Faisal in October 1918. He
rode in followed by 1500 Arab horsemen amid scenes of great
rejoicing and enthusiasm. To Faisal and his father, Husain,
Damascus was the goal of their national ambitions. Surely it would
mark the beginning of a revived Arab empire. They had a great
shock. General Allenby also entered Damascus and told Faisal that
(according to the Sykes–Picot agreement) he had instructions to
allow the French to take control and become the protecting power.
The French government had already appointed a High Commissioner for Palestine and Syria, none other than Monsieur Picot,
which showed the way their thoughts were tending. In theory,
France had also promised to support an independent state in the
area. When Faisal protested against any French presence, Allenby
insisted that his orders had to be obeyed and that he must accept the
situation. Nevertheless, Faisal was permitted to establish an 'Arab
Military Government for all Syria' in an area that was not precisely
defined. This would be, he declared, tempting fate, a constitutional
government which would be 'fully and absolutely independent'.
Faisal continued to put his faith in the impending Versailles peace

conference, where he trusted that the Allies would honour their pledges.

During his visit to Britain and France to discuss the future of the Arab territories he came face to face with the brutal realities of great power politics. The British 'advised' him to accept French control in Syria as he was told that Britain had no intention of opposing France over Syrian questions. Faisal was totally outmanoeuvred and the French treated him with 'studied contempt'. The fiery French prime minister, Clemenceau, known in friendly fashion as 'the tiger', thoroughly distrusted Faisal and his British adviser, Lawrence. Faisal was allowed to address the conference and he repeated that the aim of the Arabs was complete unity and that Syria was quite capable of managing its own affairs. These words fell on deaf ears[3] and, despite some rather tense Anglo-French rivalry, when the Allies met later at the San Remo conference in April 1920 they established the system of mandates whereby certain European powers were to be entrusted under the League of Nations with the government of former imperial territories to prepare them for eventual self-rule. Thus the future of most Arab countries was disposed of. Palestine, Jordan and Iraq were given to Britain, Syria and Lebanon (separated from each other) to France.

Syria had experienced only a very short period of self-government after Faisal's arrival in Damascus in October 1918. An interim arrangement, it faced many problems, including the fact that Faisal with his supporters was a Hashimite from Hijaz attempting to rule Syrians who were not all willing to recognize his authority. Breathing over their shoulders were the French eagerly eyeing new colonial acquisitions. The Syrian economy, agriculture and industry were badly damaged by the war and disruption in the countryside led to large-scale immigration into Damascus.

Once the Ottomans had gone, Syrian towns were left under the loose control of those members of local notable families who had previously acted as intermediaries under Ottoman rule. They had been pro-Turkish and supporters of the Ottoman attempts at reform. During the war the Turks had behaved badly towards the Syrians, accusing them of treason and of supporting the Allies. Several had been executed which caused bitter resentment. These actions and the collapse of the empire left the notables with no option but to switch to the cause of Arabism, of supporting the establishment of as large an independent Arab state as possible.

They were anti-Hashimite in feeling and yet realized that to gain any control and to retain their socio-economic position they would have to co-operate with Faisal who was backed by the British. On the other hand, Faisal could not rule without their support. In competition with older notables there emerged a group of younger nationalists eager for power, who were destined to play an important future role. Syrian politics were developing apace with the formation of political groupings which demanded total independence for all Arab countries. The French were not prepared to tolerate any demands from these new politicians or from Faisal himself. By October 1919 Syria was in a parlous state. British occupying troops had gone leaving a gap the French were waiting to fill. Faisal had accepted the arrangement at the peace conference whereby Lebanon was separated from Syria and there followed anti-Hashimite demonstrations in Damascus. Syrian politicians criticized Faisal and rejected the agreement. This was too much for General Gouraud, commander of the French army in the Levant, who sent an ultimatum to Faisal demanding the dismissal of the Syrian 'extremists'. Faisal had to concur and the population rose in protest. The French then decided to intervene. In July 1920 a group of Hashimite soldiers and Syrian irregulars clashed with the advancing French army at Maisalun outside Damascus. The outcome was never in doubt. The Syrians were routed and Faisal and his Hashimites were forced to leave the country. The short-lived Arab kingdom fell and Damascus passed under French control for the next two decades. In colonial history 20 years is a short time, yet they were years which deeply marked Syrian history.

The British felt vaguely responsible and placed Faisal on the throne of Iraq where he ruled with some success until his death in 1933. The other Hashimite brother, Abdallah, was made ruler of Transjordan. The father, Husain, was abandoned by the British and he left the Hijaz ignominiously in 1924 after which the Saudis incorporated the area into the kingdom of Saudi Arabia. Husain died in Amman in 1931 thoroughly (and rightly) disillusioned with the British.

Syria under the French to 1939

Syria was the last of a long line of territories to fall into the orbit of the French empire which had grown up alongside and in conflict with the British. Nationalism was the prime motive of France in expanding its colonies; clashes with the British raised this interest into a question of national honour. France had lost India (at the end of the eighteenth century) and Canada (1763) to the British, had withdrawn from the Anglo-French expedition to Egypt (1882) and had been halted by the British on the frontier of Sudan (1896). On the other hand Algeria had been occupied in 1830, Tunisia in 1881 and Morocco 1912. By 1914 all the North African coast was in European hands; Syria, Lebanon and Palestine remained to be grabbed. Because of previous activity there by French missionaries, teachers and businessmen, Syria was looked upon as a region of special interest, and the interests France wanted there far exceeded those it already had. The area around Alexandretta on the northern Syrian coast (called Cilicia) was particularly desirable. It was an oil pipe-line terminal, the port for Aleppo and a terminus for desert caravans. As a member of the Chamber of Deputies declared in June 1920, 'The possession [of Alexandretta] is essential to the future of France!'[4] The French had gained the right to participate in the dismemberment of the Ottoman Empire by fighting in the war and laid claim to Cilicia together with Syria and Lebanon.

The French entered Syria as conquerors, not as enlightened guests bearing the banner of the League of Nations, pledged to help and advise a state recognized as independent. Almost the first words of Gouraud in Beirut in 1919 were, 'We come to you as descendants of the Crusaders'. Few Syrians had much faith in French good intentions. Officially the Mandate bound France to provide an organic statute for Syria and in particular to safeguard local autonomies. It gave to France control of foreign affairs but no monopoly of internal development. There thus seemed to be limits on French action. The Arabs were less sure. One Arab historian bluntly called the mandate system a substitute for colonialism. Even a French publication noted in 1939, 'In the opinion of the majority of the French, France "possesses" Syria. Its duty is to administer and preserve French interests there. One does not negotiate with colonies. One keeps them and protects them against outside threats. One administers them. And that is all . . . For the majority of Frenchmen in effect our *mandate* in Syria is hardly more than a fiction.'[5] French school textbooks too gave the impression that Syria was purely and simply incorporated into the French colonial possessions. This was precisely the view of most Syrians. The effect of such a belief on them made relations with the French difficult and delicate. They felt humiliated and mistrustful and this feeling increased their determination to put an end to the occupation as soon as possible. The French sense of superiority and their often unthinking behaviour infuriated the Syrians. The High Commissioners held all the power and the first three were generals who had gained colonial experience in Africa. To run the administration behind a Syrian façade they appointed French officials and advisers who were often of mediocre ability, corrupt and ignorant of Arabic and local conditions. The military officers from the African colonies tended to be autocratic. The Special (intelligence) Services were a law unto themselves, abusing their office, with arbitrary arrests, imprisonment and deportations. Their activities worried the Permanent Mandates Commission in Geneva and were even criticized in the French Chamber of Deputies. The Mandates Commission likened the powers of the commissioner to those of a 'chief of a foreign army occupying a foreign country' – which again was a very close approach to the truth. In fact, military expenditure in Syria was ten times that on civilian projects and France had always to use military force (or the threat of it) to maintain its authority.

One of the first acts of the Mandate authority was to split up the area under its control. In April 1920 Greater Lebanon was created to take in a large number of Muslim inhabitants at the expense of Syria. This move complicated the problem of self-government in Lebanon (and does so to this day) and aroused considerable hostility in Syria. Since that time relations between Syria and Lebanon have been special as Syria has never recognized the partition. Aleppo and Damascus were divided into two states and in March 1921 the Druze mountain was recognized as separate. The territory of the Alawis around Latakia was declared another separate state in 1922. Thus the French mandated area was split into five separate areas to the annoyance of many of the inhabitants. This blatant policy of divide and rule was amended somewhat in 1924 when Aleppo and Damascus were amalgamated into the state of Syria.

Syrian nationalist politics developed slowly under the French as the politicians had to reorganize themselves in the new situation after the war. It took time to adjust to a French Christian rather than an Ottoman Muslim government. In 1925 the French decided to allow the formation of political parties and a group of nationalists banded together in the People's Party led by Abd al-Rahman

Shahbandar[6] and Faris al-Khuri[7] who had both served in Faisal's government. The aims of the party were Syrian unity and an independent state. To achieve these aims it followed that French rule and the policy of dividing the area had to be opposed. The programme of the People's Party reflected the interests of its founders – the urban bourgeoisie. They wanted not only unity and independence but also modernizing reforms, the development of industry and education. The leaders were still the traditional élite of Syrian society, national not radical, who wished to maintain their positions in a new Syria.

French rule inevitably caused considerable unrest which on occasions broke out into open revolt. The most serious of these was in the Druze area during the years 1925–7. The Druzes like many mountain people are proud and fiercely independent. Resentment of the clumsy French attempts to administer them drove them to take up arms. The fighting began with a disastrous defeat of the French in which they suffered heavy casualties and losses of arms and ammunition. A raid was made on Damascus in August 1924 which the French believed was backed by the People's Party. Six of its members were arrested but Shahbandar escaped to the Druze area where he proclaimed a Syrian national government. The 'rebels' put forward a number of demands including unification and French evacuation, which the French rejected out of hand. The fighting continued and spread to other parts of the country. It was in many ways a typical guerrilla war in the sense of a large well-equipped army fighting smaller groups often in hilly country.

By the summer of 1927 the French had succeeded in bringing hostilities to an end, although their prestige was severely dented. An amnesty was proclaimed for the rebels. Negotiations over a constitution for the country began shakily between the French and Syrian leaders. The French gave the President of the Syrian Council of Ministers the task of forming a government which would call elections for an Assembly to draft the constitution. Elections in 1928 resulted in an Assembly dominated by nationalists. The President of the Assembly was Hashim al-Atasi,[8] a leading nationalist politician. The proposed constitution, which contained clauses to which the French objected (for example 'Syrian territories constitute an indivisible political unity'), was rejected by High Commissioner Ponsot. The Assembly in turn rejected his amendments. Ponsot then issued his own constitution and dissolved the Assembly. In fact Ponsot's constitution admitted the 'indivisible' political unity of Syria but also mentioned the obligations of France with regard to the country. It was a French document put into force by the French.

Further elections were held on its basis in 1932 when a constitutional government came into office led by members of the National Bloc, a grouping founded by former members of Faisal's Arab government and considered as successors to the People's Party whose leaders had been exiled for their part in the revolt. They tried to re-negotiate with the French and once again clashed over how much 'rule' the Syrians could actually exercise in their own country. The French were unwilling to concede all that the Syrians demanded. In 1933 negotiations began over a Franco-Syrian treaty which would formally regulate relations between the two sides. Although the proposed treaty was based on the Anglo-Iraqi treaty by which Iraq was granted independence and admitted to the League of Nations, it contained certain clauses (dealing with sovereignty and unity) unacceptable to the nationalists. It raised such a storm in the Assembly that Ponsot was compelled to suspend it. When he retired later that year the question of Syrian independence was no nearer to solution.

The new High Commissioner, de Martel, decided to try new, tougher tactics. He forced the prime minister to accept the treaty and when the Assembly once again rejected it he suspended it for an indefinite period. By taking over most powers himself he made the prime minister appear a mere tool in his hands and very unpopular with the nationalist politicians, who held aloof from the taint of collaboration. Early in 1936 opposition broke out when de Martel ordered the exile of the leader of the National Bloc. There was a general strike and in clashes between the police and demonstrators several people were killed. By March de Martel seemed to have capitulated and invited the nationalists to negotiate a new treaty in Paris. Relations were difficult at first until a Socialist government was elected in France under Léon Blum, who was more favourable towards compromise, and in September a Franco-Syrian treaty of alliance was signed.

At home a new Syrian cabinet was formed which included most nationalist politicians who were to play important roles in Syrian politics – Jamil Mardam[9] as Prime Minister, Saadallah Jabiri,[10] Minister of the Interior, Shukri al-Quwatli,[11] Finance and Defence. Faris al-Khuri was elected Speaker of the Assembly and Hashim al-Atasi President of the State. The pattern, or at least the personalities of Syrian politics, was now set for the next generation. Relations with the French, which should have improved considerably, were soured by rumours that French colonial officials in Paris were trying to reassert their influence against Blum and to have the treaty repudiated by the French Chamber of Deputies. These rumours helped to confirm the deep suspicions about French good faith.

Another matter which infuriated the Syrians was the French decision to cede the area of Alexandretta to Turkey. This was a grave inconvenience to the inhabitants of Aleppo and its hinterland who had had direct access to the sea through the port of Alexandretta. Syrians claimed – and still claim – that the area is Arab and an integral part of Syria. Nationalist leaders could hardly have prevented this French move but nevertheless lost popularity because of it. Their helplessness was underlined when the French Chamber refused to ratify the treaty in 1939. The people turned to rioting and demonstrations to express their discontent. Several new governments were tried to little avail. The French responded harshly with military suppression and mass arrests; the constitution was suspended, the Assembly dissolved and virtual direct rule brought in. This meant that 20 years of French rule had led almost nowhere. The Syrians, on the basis of very little experience had had to establish a government, a parliament and an administration. Fighting the French had distorted and largely nullified these efforts. A small number of politicians had come to the fore in the new situation and had gained some experience. Everything was then changed by the outbreak of the Second World War.

The Second World War

Once again a war between the European powers radically changed the course of Syrian history. Again a significant part of that war was fought in the Middle East. For Syria the most important fact was the early defeat of France by the Germans. How would this affect the French position in Syria? The answer was complicated by the formation of the two Frances – the Vichy government to administer France jointly with the Nazis, and the Free French to continue to fight led by the young, irritating and immensely self-confident General de Gaulle. He fled to Britain where singlemindedly he began to organize French resistance. His problem was that he had to rely on British help and could do little alone – this was wounding to his pride and made him a prickly ally. Churchill especially had to suffer him and together they had to face major problems, including the future of the French empire.

In Syria the Vichy authorities were still in charge. Some Syrians began to wonder whether their future lay with the victorious Axis powers and the Germans became more active in Syria. In April the Vichy government withdrew from the League of Nations thus legally terminating the Mandate – the French therefore remained only as an occupying power. To put an end to the ambiguity and to forestall further German or pro-German moves in June 1941 British troops joined those of the Free French to invade Syria on the pretext that the Vichy had allowed German planes to land there. Within one month the Anglo-French forces had occupied the whole of the country. This did not ease matters. The British and French had to try to co-operate in running the country. In the long term they failed. The British sent Major-General Louis Spears to head a mission to the country and eventually to become First Minister to the Levant States. As such he had to bear the full brunt of French resentment. In the end he felt that he had been made the whipping boy for all the French frustrations. In his defence he wrote, 'My own dispassionate view is that the Levant was lost [by the French] because of the bullying, hectoring and dictatorial methods of General de Gaulle'.[12]

Churchill was caught up in a constant dispute. In a secret interview between him and de Gaulle in 1941 he said that 'he had witnessed with very great sorrow the deterioration in General de Gaulle's attitude towards Britain . . . [he] had throughout his recent travels left a trail of Anglophobia behind him'. Churchill insisted that

> Britain had no desire whatever to supplement France. Clearly the security of our position in the Arab world involved a transfer of many of the functions previously exercised by France in Syria to the Syrians themselves. The position of France in respect to Syria after the war would be different from that which obtained before – because France would have voluntarily transferred powers to the Syrians. This was essential. The Arabs saw no sense in driving out the Vichy French only to be placed under the control of the Free French. They desired their independence and had been promised it.[13]

To this de Gaulle replied that he had himself promised Syria independence. In fact on the eve of the Anglo-French invasion General Catroux, de Gaulle's representative in Cairo, in his name promised Syria and Lebanon unconditional independence and the right to unite if they so wished. As the Free French were not a government and de Gaulle no more than the self-appointed head of a movement it was agreed that for the French promise to be of any value it had to be guaranteed by Britain. This was done officially and eventually led to the end of the French in Syria.

Spears's view was that the French did little to make themselves popular during the war. 'With the exception of the religious and educational foundations in the Levant the French, who could so easily have been liked, managed to make themselves utterly disliked and feared.'[14] When de Gaulle came to Syria 'he tended to assume the attitude of a dictator and a sovereign returning to his state'.[15] Tension between the British and French continued. The French insisted on trying to run the country themselves, refusing British help although there were few competent men available. Again, according to Spears, 'General Catroux, aping his master, behaved as an absolute dictator. The type of man he appointed to responsible posts often enjoyed the worst possible reputation.'

It also seemed to Spears that 'the Free French and General Catroux had no intention whatsoever of giving the states their promised freedom'. This was too much and under British pressure the French restored the constitution, elections were held and the National Bloc won an overwhelming victory. Shukri al-Quwatli was elected president. The French claimed that the British had influenced the result and that Spears had been 'riding about the mountains on a white horse distributing gold'! In fact, because of the presence of a large British army of occupation stationed everywhere, it is probable that the people had felt free to express their real opinions.

The nationalist government announced its intention of terminating the Mandate and of abolishing French controls. In 1944 the Soviet Union and the United States recognized Syria and in February 1945 Syria declared war on Germany. The French refused to give in completely and demanded a treaty guaranteeing economic and military rights. Early in 1945 de Gaulle saw a last opportunity of trying to save the French position in Syria. He brought troops in but the Syrians refused to discuss under duress. There were anti-French disturbances and the French bombarded

Damascus causing 2500 casualties. It was the situation of 1920 repeating itself; this time it ended differently. The British Commander-in-Chief rushed troops to Syria and took over. As Spears concluded, not without a touch of malice, 'The French had the humiliation of being escorted out of Damascus by British armed forces'. At the United Nations, France was compelled to complete its withdrawal from Syria in April 1946. Independence had been finally won.

Notes

1   Russia also took part in the original negotiations but dropped out after 1917.
2   Named after the British and French officials, Sir Mark Sykes and M. Georges Picot, who drafted the text.
3   The United States in their turn distrusted the imperialist powers. They sent a Commission of Enquiry to Syria in 1919 consisting of Dr Henry King and Charles Crane. They reported to US President Wilson that Syria should not be split up and that a mandate should be given either to the United States or Britain, in no case to France because of a general aversion to that country.
4   J. Henry-Haye and P. Vienot, *Les relations de la France et de la Syrie mars 1939* (Paris, 1939), p. 13.
5   ibid.
6   A Western-trained doctor from Damascus who had been active politically before the war.
7   A Christian lawyer who had worked in the British Consulate in Damascus. Both men were to play leading roles in Syrian politics.
8   A member of an important Homs family. He had been Prime Minister in Faisal's government.
9   A member of an old, politically active landowning family from Damascus.
10 A leading family from Aleppo.
11 Belonging to a family with the same background as Mardam.
12 Spears Papers, Memorandum 14 April 1954 (in the Middle East Centre, St Antony's College, Oxford).
13 ibid., Record of a meeting between Churchill and de Gaulle, 12 September 1941.
14 Spears Memorandum.
15 ibid.

3 Independence 1945–1970

The ills which are playing havoc with the nation . . .
can no longer be cured by the ability of politicians.
(M. Aflaq)

The Old Guard and Coups 1945–1956

In 1945 a Syrian memorandum to the United Nations described
recent Syrian history thus: 'In 1943 a representative and constitutional government was set up . . . Since then the national government has proceeded with rapid strides towards the firm establishment of its existence internally as well as externally.' In fact
independent Syria still had to face many problems, not just those of
a country in the immediate postwar era but also of a state tasting
independence for the first time without many settled and tried
institutions. The energy dissipated in fighting the French had now to
be channelled into more productive areas. Important economic,
political and social decisions concerning the future were necessary,
yet the politicians entrusted with making them were untried leaders
who tended to waste their talents in trying to retain personal power.
They split into two main groupings rather than parties, although
they bore party labels. The nationalist leaders had originally
banded together under the umbrella of the National Bloc. Now they
split into the National Party which included men such as Quwatli,
Jamil Mardam and Faris al-Khuri whose support came mainly from
Damascus. In 1947 opponents to this group began to come together
in a new People's Party, which represented interests from Aleppo
and the north of the country and also gained the support of the Atasi
family whose power base was in Homs.

A development of overwhelming importance during this period
was the emergence of a political party with a clear ideology and
political programme – the Baath party, founded by two young
Syrian nationalists, Michel Aflaq and Salah Bitar. The ideology of
the Baath will be discussed in a later chapter. Its importance here
lies in the fact that its founders were nationalists of a new

generation, tied neither to families nor place, who had espoused the cause of a wider Arab nationalism that was to have profound consequences for the future of Syria. In 1947 the Baath were not strong enough to act independently and threw in their lot with the People's Party. In their view the National Party was bankrupt and out of touch with the demands of younger Syrians for reform in various areas of national life. The People's Party, although not of a mind with the Baath, was at least in opposition.

Another important political actor came to the fore at this time, Akram Hawrani from Hama. In the 1930s he had been a militant in revolt against the French mandate and led a youth movement of fascist tendencies. He took part in guerrilla attacks and in 1945 occupied the citadel in Hama and expelled the French garrison. He founded his own Arab Socialist Party although his views tended to move towards those of the Baath. His support came from some younger members of the army and from peasants and villagers around Hama. He was a man of action rather than ideas, belligerent and energetic, and was to play an important role in Syrian politics.

These politicians of the newly independent Syria held elections in July 1947. They were a means of establishing a kind of political legitimacy once the French had left and were relatively free in a country where parliamentary democracy was a fragile plant. The opposition won 33 seats, the National Party 24 and the others (independent) more than 50. These latter represented the traditional power bases of landowners, merchants, tribal and minority leaders, heads of the largest families – in fact the notables of earlier times. That this group formed the largest single bloc showed that local and old loyalties remained strong. The nationalists took office, with Quwatli President, Jamil Mardam Prime Minister and Faris al-Khuri President of the Chamber of Deputies. Once back in power they seemed to be mainly intent on maintaining their own position and feathering their own nests. Critics have been hard on these men – 'tired politicians' – 'part of the whole creaking network of family patronage and administrative venality'.[1] Members of this old guard would retort that they were nationalist leaders attempting to run the country to the best of their ability. They were, in any case, older men who had known Ottoman rule, who had struggled through the French occupation and who were to taste few of the fruits of a hard-won independence.

War in Palestine

The whole Syrian structure – and indeed the whole Arab world – was severely shaken by events in Palestine. In 1920 the British government had accepted the Mandate for Palestine from the League of Nations by which it undertook to fulfil the promises of the Balfour Declaration and to prepare the country for independence. The next twenty-seven years saw a series of doomed British attempts to accommodate the claim of both Jews and Arabs to inhabit and govern the same small country. By 1947 Britain admitted that no solution seemed possible and announced its intention of abandoning the country. In September the Arab League[2] decided to resist by force a United Nations plan for partition. The Arab states believed that their armies would easily defeat the small number of armed Jewish settlers. Under their leader, David Ben Gurion, these settlers proclaimed in May 1948 the foundation of the state of Israel in those areas they controlled when the British officially terminated the Mandate.

The Arab armies entered Palestine that same month. Splendid speeches were made by Arab politicians who led the public to expect an easy and speedy victory. But the reality was very different. The armies were not unified, were poorly equipped, ill-organized and over-confident. Within a few days it was clear that the new state was not going to be destroyed. There were charges of corruption in the Syrian and Egyptian armies. Weapons were ineffective, and the Arabs were facing opponents for whom it was win or die. Many of them had fled from Nazi Europe and Israel was their last refuge. They fought tenaciously to preserve and expand their territory. For the younger Arab officers defeat was a disgrace and it marked both in Egypt and Syria the beginning of the end of the old regimes. The officers returned home humiliated, blaming the old politicians and the old system for the débâcle. In Egypt the Free Officers took four years to plan and execute the coup which swept away the old regime. In Syria the young officers assumed the role of guardians of their country's prestige and like army officers elsewhere believed that only they embodied the legitimacy and honour of the state.

The First Army Coup

Discontent fanned by strikes and riots spread throughout the country. The prime minister, Jamil Mardam, resigned in December 1948. No politician was really able to cope with this situation of discontent which had come about so soon after independence. But in Syria neither was there any Jamal Abd al-Nasser waiting to mastermind a military takeover. Instead the army chief of staff, Husni al-Zaim, decided to seize power. He was a rather second-rate man whose past had not been blameless. He was certainly not an austere, remote Nasser. His coup was, however, well organized; the old politicans were arrested and the army seized strategic positions. The old guard had no way of combating the takeover and retired from the scene. They had tried and failed to run the country in a democratic fashion. The strains imposed in particular by the Palestine catastrophe were too great. They represented nationalist liberal ideals whereas the young men coming to power represented more radical trends.

Zaim's rule lasted a scant four and a half months. He made an attempt to put Syria on a new path by strengthening the army and modernizing various sectors of Syrian life. He could not contain his political ambitions, however, and soon alienated his supporters. He had broken the mould of Syrian politics and ensured that the army henceforth was never again far from the political stage. In seizing on the resentment over Palestine he also ensured that the issue would remain central to Syrian politics. Zaim's over-ambitiousness led to his downfall. The next coup in August 1949 was led by ever more self-righteous men who accused the 'tyrant Zaim and his servile clique'[3] of committing innumerable crimes against the state. The new leader, Colonel Hinnawi, rather strangely brought back the politicians and asked them to run the country. They tried to do so until the next coup in December 1949.

The Shishakli Coup

Hinnawi is not much remembered and was soon overshadowed by Colonel Adib al-Shishakli whose regime lasted much longer – some four years. His coup followed now established lines – seizure of strategic points, arrest of so-called opponents and the branding of those removed as traitors and conspirators. Shishakli was a native of Hama and had known Hawrani in his youth. They had fought together against the French and Zionists and together they engineered the coup of 1949. They had some ideas on the future of

Syria, not many on how to put them into practice. As men from Hama they were outsiders to the politicians of Damascus and they had to inch their way forwards towards political acceptance. They believed in power and yet left rule in the first years to the politicians. In fact Shishakli was a cautious man, perhaps unwilling to expose himself too soon to public assessment. The politicians tended to carry on in their old ways, perhaps unwilling to admit that the army now held real power. The squabbles they had among themselves (National against People's Party) weakened them in face of a growing power. The Baath party during this period was biding its time, content to watch the older politicians destroying themselves.

Political infighting seemed to leave little time for Syria's pressing internal problems. External affairs of the period of the early 1950s included the questions of Syria's relations with other Arab states (particularly the possibility of union with Iraq), feuding on the frontier with Israel, and the West's attempt to bring Syria into defence alliances aimed against the Soviet Union. This latter move aroused great indignation in Syria where it was seen as a European attempt to draw the country into an imperialist network against an imaginary enemy. Few Syrians wanted to welcome back Western 'protection' after having so recently ousted France. There developed a current of neutralism (later called non-alignment) which sought good relations with all those states which respected Syrian independence, closer relations with the Soviet Union and arms from the Eastern bloc which would allow Syria more flexibility. The Americans in particular saw this trend (as in Egypt) as the growth of anti-Americanism and a move towards Communism.

The older politicians continued the uphill struggle to retain power in the face of the army. While the new leaders, Hawrani and the Baath, were not unhappy to see the decline of their older rivals, they did not welcome the army monopoly of power. The Baath was eager to run the country itself and to put its own ideology into practice. Shishakli in December 1951 decided that the time had come to consolidate his position and in a second coup took all political power for the army, installing a colonel as prime minister and head of state. Shishakli was Syria's first real military dictator and his 'tenure of power was marked with far-reaching implications'[4] for the following period of Syrian history. His first task was to improve and modernize the army. This had at least two results. The younger officers who enlisted became accustomed to the army participating in political life and were ever more reluctant to confine their interest to the barracks. Also, as the army became stronger the ambition to destroy Israel and recapture Palestine became more deeply rooted and the obsession and end of all military improvement.

Military regimes are run on military principles – discipline, obedience, conformity. Soldiers should not question orders or even the wisdom of their superiors. Parliamentary democracies are founded on questions and doubts about the wisdom of leaders. Shishakli tried to control Syria. Supervision of foreigners, education and religious activities were tightened up. The activities of many sections of society were curbed and the Muslim Brothers were banned (see p. 83). Members of some minority groups who had lived peaceably in Syria began to feel that their position was threatened. This imposition of a heavy hand was both a result of army discipline and of over-reaction to the demands of running a state. The army newly in power still had to prove itself in office. Hawrani provided some of the ideological basis of the programme that Shishakli was attempting to put into operation. One of the more radical ideas was a rather unsuccessful attempt at the redistribution of land.

Shishakli's heavy hand brought a reaction. Arrests were made of any who criticized his actions and Aflaq, Bitar and Hawrani himself fled to avoid arrest. As he became more autocratic he alienated his one-time supporters. In fact he achieved the unique distinction of uniting all the opposition against him and in July 1953 they banded together to depose him. It is interesting that the opposition was locally based – in Aleppo, Hama and the Druze mountain. Once again it was the army which came to depose him. Shishakli and his clique were accused of bringing shame and disgrace[5] to the country and the army. The military, or at least part of it, acted as self-appointed guardians of the public conscience. It rose in revolt and Shishakli's support melted away. He was forced to resign in February 1954. He seemed to have no stomach for a fight and no wish to plunge the country into bloodshed. Shishakli left Syria in a state of confusion. He had brought the army into politics but had not established a stable or recognized system of government.

What was to be the next move in political life? Party politics came back to play a role. The period of military dictatorship was ostensibly written out of the history books. Reasonably free elections were held and a number of parties put up candidates, including the old National and People's Parties, the Baath and the

Communists. Several old politicians were still around, including Quwatli, and newer ones including Bitar and Hawrani of the Baath. In fact independent candidates won a majority (64) followed by the People's Party (30), Baath (22) and National (19). The most important aspect of these results was the emergence of the Baath party as a force in Syrian politics. Their ideology, or at least a form of it, was to influence political life henceforth. This is not to say that politics became purely ideological as personalities continued to play an important role. In fact, the new prime minister, a member of the old guard, Faris al-Khuri, was unable to persuade members of the Baath to join his government. He and his colleagues had to face a new era in Syrian life in which there were two influential factors. One was the growth of Soviet activity in the Middle East; the other, perhaps even more important, was the rise of Jamal Abd al-Nasser as ruler of Egypt. Nasser was the symbol of the new Arab world – a young army officer who had removed an old and corrupt regime, who had put an end to the British occupation of his country and who was then able to pursue a more independent policy *vis-à-vis* the West by relying on Russian support. He rejected Western alliances and came to be regarded as both an Arab and a non-aligned leader. There was no one of comparable stature in any other Arab country. In a sense other Arab leaders, until his death in 1970, had to act very much under his shade. During this time Syria and Egypt were drawing closer together; they both opposed Western pacts, both sought arms from Russia and both had the defeat of Israel as a major policy aim.

An immediate practical result of this convergence of aims was the signing of a military pact between the two countries in October 1955. An Egyptian officer, Mahmud Riyad (later to become Secretary-General of the Arab League), had been appointed ambassador to Syria in the spring of 1955 and according to his memoirs it was he who urged Nasser to sign the pact although he 'was reluctant at first, in view of his apprehension that the differences between the Syrian parties might lead to obstructing the successful conclusion of such an agreement'.[7] Characteristic, however, of the publicly expressed feelings of optimism at the time and also of the trend of Nasser's thought was the speech he made at the signing ceremony:

This agreement is the prelude to a new future. History shows that if Syria and Egypt unite they will protect the Eastern world from

all dangers that may threaten it. That is what took place at the
time of the Crusades . . . Today Syria and Egypt will protect the
Arab world against Zionism.[8]

The agreement did not mean that the relationship was easy.
Nasser was the dominant figure and his idea of Arab unity was unity
under his leadership. The traditions, resources and sizes of the two
countries were very different and Syria inevitably became the junior
partner. An Egyptian general, a close colleague of Nasser, Abd
al-Hakim Amir was appointed to head the joint military command.
Not much of practical value was achieved in the military field; the
symbolic significance was considerable. Riyad occupied a special
role in this relationship and established important links with the
leaders of the Baath whose ideology made it incumbent on them to
welcome and support any moves towards unity. Indeed they went
further, compelled by the logic of their beliefs, and called for the
complete union of the two states. The growing strength and
popularity of the Baath party ensured that Syria could not really be
ruled without them. A shaky government fell in June 1956 and a
new one of national unity could only be formed with Baath support;
Salah Bitar became foreign minister. Aflaq, the party leader,
declared, 'We entered the national coalition government on the
condition that it should undertake to achieve federation between
Egypt and Syria, because we knew that national rule . . . means
postponing or narrowing the internal battle'.[9] The Syrian Chamber
of Deputies backed these feelings and passed a resolution wishing
the government 'success in following this holy path bringing us in
the near future to the goal awaited by the Arab peoples in all their
countries'.[10]

Suez and the Road to Union

The reality of politics in Syria was rather less noble. There was
rivalry among politicians and between them and the army. The
absence of an established stable system led to competition and
jockeying for power. An outside event emanating from Egypt
concentrated Syrian attention. In July 1956 Nasser nationalized the
Suez Canal which had until then been run by an international
company based in Paris. Nasser's move was hailed as another blow
for Arab independence and warmly supported by Syria. There was

little Syria could do practically when, later, Britain, France and Israel invaded Egypt in a vain attempt to topple Nasser. Riyad reported:

> I was invited . . . to attend a stormy meeting of the Syrian Cabinet of Ministers, who insisted that Syria was under a national and historical obligation to enter the war on the side of Egypt, whatever the consequences, to convince them that it was Egypt that declined this offer. The following day I was visited by a number of army commanders . . . and we decided that the pipelines owned by a British oil company passing through Syria should be blown up.[11]

This second 'Arab' war against Israel was one in which the Syrians did not really participate. They were held back by Egypt which believed that if Syria attacked Israel it would itself be invaded by Britain and France. However, Syrian sympathy for Egypt's plight brought the two countries closer together.

There were problems on the path towards union caused by outside interference. The Suez crisis had brought the United States permanently into Middle Eastern affairs for two reasons: the power of Britain and France was waning leaving, in American eyes, a vacuum to be filled; and the Soviet Union was perceived by the Americans to be expanding its influence in the area to a dangerous extent. President Eisenhower in January 1957 proclaimed a doctrine by which aid was offered to those countries in the Middle East believed to be threatened by international communism. Nasser rejected this doctrine outright and Syria, despite pressure from Saudi Arabia which had accepted it, was struggling to reject it. Although Syria did not feel threatened by Russia, the United States regarded it as a Soviet satellite as early as 1957 and has continued to do so. Syria resisted American pressure to accept the Eisenhower offer and stressed once again its desire for union with Egypt.

Politically Syria was having a bad time. There were different paths for the country to follow and no consensus on which to choose. Without strong political institutions, slogans and propaganda took their place. The appeal of Nasser as leader tended to be seen as the solution to all their problems. His popularity was a threat to Arab regimes everywhere. In Syria the Baath saw him both as a foundation for their grand dream of Arab unity and as a support for their own power at home, yet Nasser was a pragmatic leader wary of rash ideological moves. Syrian army officers also began to court him in his role as a successful army leader who had rid himself of civilian politicians. But the army, like the politicians, was split by rivalries and enmities. In a surprising move the Baath turned to those members of the army sympathetic to it to encourage them to go to Cairo and demand union with Egypt. The surprise was that an army delegation did go to Cairo in January 1958 to ask for such a union without the authority of the civilian government. The foreign minister, Bitar, was immediately told to go to Cairo to discover what they were up to. As a Baathi committed to union he promptly supported the officers.

Nasser was in a strong position *vis-à-vis* his Syrian petitioners. He was the only possible leader of the proposed union; the Syrians were weak, divided and leaderless. He could, therefore, impose his own conditions. He demanded total union, the abolition of all political parties except his own National Union and the Syrian army's abstention from politics. It was ironic that the Baath agreed to the second condition and the army officers to the third. They had no option. On 1 February 1958 Presidents Nasser and Quwatli proclaimed the formation of the United Arab Republic. It was a move into the unknown made in the heat of enthusiasm. The joint communiqué declared: 'In proclaiming these decisions, the partici-pants feel great pride and overwhelming joy in having assisted in taking this positive step on the road to Arab unity and solidarity.' Nasser said: 'Today Arab nationalism is not just a matter of slogans and shouts; it has become an actual reality, today the Arab people of Syria have united with the Arab people of Egypt to form the United Arab Republic.' President Quwatli publicly suppressed any misgivings he might have had and replied enthusiastically:

> This day is one of the most memorable days in history. It is the reward for our glorious struggle of the past, a hope in the future of the Arab peoples . . . In proclaiming the union of these two beloved Arab countries, of these two long-struggling nations into one homeland . . . we undertook no new or arbitrary task. Rather did we restore the normal order of things.[12]

A referendum in the two countries approved the union and Nasser was elected president with a 99.9 per cent majority. The provisional constitution of the UAR made clear just how much power he would have: 'The President is the Head of State; Supreme Commander of the [joint] Armed Forces; he may appoint one or more Vice-Presidents, and he may relieve them of their posts; he appoints and dismisses Ministers and has the right to dissolve the National Assembly.' The UAR was to consist of two regions – the northern and the southern – with Cairo as capital. And here was the root of future problems – the unequal relationship and Egyptian insensitivity. For the time being, however, the atmosphere was heady.

Nasser visited Damascus and was given an overwhelming welcome. Thousands came into the streets to greet him, the most popular Arab leader ever, and Arabism was at its zenith. Underneath problems were already present. The Syrians are a proud and sensitive people and Nasser was planning to impose on them a police and army regime as his solution to the problems of the union. There was no possibility of merging the two political systems – Syria with its instability and fragmentation, Egypt with its one leader and party. In addition to the dissolution of Syrian political parties, army officers were dismissed and Egyptian security officials sent to Syria. Thus Nasser attempted to impose his will, paying little attention to Syrian sensitivities and attitudes. He believed that his own popular appeal would guarantee success.

The Syrians proved to be difficult bedfellows. The Baath obviously could not assume exclusive leadership and in October 1958 in a new cabinet 14 out of 21 ministers (including the most important) were allotted to Egyptians. Nasser's other moves alienated a considerable section of the population – landowners who disliked the plans for agrarian reform, politicians who lost power, businessmen and the army. He realized that things were going wrong and in October 1958 he sent his colleague Abd al-Hakim Amir as governor with orders to try to conciliate Syrian opinion. The Baath were still smarting and resigned from the government in December. Nasser used Abd al-Hamid Sarraj, the tough Syrian intelligence chief, as his strong man, making him Minister of the Interior and President of the Executive Council of the National Union – the organization founded to replace political parties. Sarraj was dedicated to Nasser; he was efficient and ruthless, and earned widespread unpopularity. Nasser tried to silence every centre of political power and Sarraj supported him with a strong security network. Discontent grew, especially in the army, members of which began to plot to take Syria out of the UAR. Amir attempted to halt some of Sarraj's more excessive police methods, but it was too late. A Syrian general later complained that 'Every Egyptian officer during the union acted as if he were Jamal Abd al-Nasser, and Syrian officers were so demoralized that . . . they felt no incentive to oppose the secession'. On 28 September 1961 army units stationed outside Damascus marched on the capital where they were joined by others and a national uprising was proclaimed. Nasser's first impulse was to resist. After reflection he realized that this would be disastrous and accepted the *infisal* – split-up. He recognized the impossibility of imposing his will on the Syrians and now spoke with hindsight of his disquiet over the hasty formation of the union.

> You know that my opinion was that unity . . . was a strenuous operation. My opinion was that preparation for it should have been made gradually over a number of years . . . but I had to submit to the popular Syrian will . . . I feel at this moment that it is not imperative that Syria remains a part of UAR, but it is imperative that Syria should remain Syria . . . National unity in Syria is a consolidation of Arab unity and true preparation for its realization.

Ex-president Quwatli succinctly summed up his feelings:

> I had hoped to share responsibility in the new state and to contribute to drawing the other [Arab] peoples into the union, but I was greatly disappointed . . . The Nasserist system relegated the majority of the population to the rank of traitors, governing by terror and trampling on the honour and dignity of citizens . . . It gave the people a National Assembly whose sole function was to approve decisions coming from above . . . They did not understand that what could be applied in Egypt could not be applied in Syria.[13]

Members of the Baath were in despair at this dismal attempt at unity and blamed all and sundry for its failure. It is not clear exactly what role they saw for themselves or how they believed they could have co-operated with Nasser. In texts issued just after the break-up their official position was stated:

> The errors of the ruling system in the UAR, however grave they may be, do not justify secession, for the fact remains that the failure of the experiment in unity is a consequence of certain

mistakes and that secession is a consequence of planning, designs and conspiracy.[14]

Now that the first and most precious experiment in unity was achieved and has failed, secession represents a new kind of fragmentation . . . [our opponents] are unifying their forces which are those of Imperialism, Zionism, Arab reactionaries and Arab haters, not only to confront any possibility of the establishment of a new unity, but also to track down the idea of unity and unitary forces and shatter them everywhere.[15]

This vision of a worldwide conspiracy against Arab unity conceded the fact that the union had also failed because of a lack of careful preparation and agreed procedures. Now Syria had to go back to governing itself on some workable basis.

Where was the basis to be found? In the first place the old conservative politicians formed a government and held an election in which they and their colleagues won a majority of seats. They then began to dismantle some of the measures (such as nationalizations) which Nasser had introduced. They had not much positive to offer and a number of cabinets floundered around looking for convincing policies. They could not disavow Arab unity although Nasser scorned them as an inconsiderable force. The Baath were in no stronger a position. The public welcome which Hawrani gave to the secession embarrassed Aflaq and Bitar. They preferred to await the next opportunity for an attempt at union and announced that they had expelled Hawrani from the party. The army was likewise suffering. There were officers who supported Nasser and others who bitterly resented the Egyptian attempts to dominate them. They quarrelled among themselves and with the civilian politicians over which policies should be followed. The quarrel between Egypt and Syria continued with each side accusing the other of interference, incitement and of serving the aims of imperialism (usually meaning making approaches to the USA). At home, Nasser decided that the way forward was to ensure the Egyptian revolution by introducing new far-reaching socialist measures which he hoped would stimulate other Arab states to follow suit.

The Syrian Coup of 1963

The military finally despaired of the fumblings of the politicians and decided once again to take matters into their own hands. A significant event in Iraq influenced the course of events in Syria. In February 1963 a coup in Baghdad brought to power the Iraqi branch of the Baath party which was naturally committed to unity and was welcomed by Nasser. Aflaq was secretary-general of the party in Damascus and he immediately opened discussions with his Iraqi colleagues. The time seemed ripe for a Baathi move in Syria. The coup came just a month later in March, carried out without violence. The politicians were too demoralized to resist. A National Revolutionary Command Council of anonymous officers and civilians assumed power and appointed a Baathi-led cabinet with Bitar as Prime Minister. The man to note is Brigadier Amin al-Hafiz who became Minister of the Interior. The council announced that it had assumed power in order to purge the crime of secession and to work for reunion. The coup was not exactly Baathi although some Baathi politicians and officers participated in it. The weakness of the Baathi politicians was demonstrated by the fact that they had to rely on army officers to obtain power. (The officers were members of a group called the Military Committee, a body affiliated to the Baath.) This relationship was to dominate Syrian politics, the army leading and politicians bending to its will while the tinge of policies was Baathist. The Baathi members of the government, as if by reflex and despite the fact that the domestic situation was in urgent need of attention, turned their eyes towards Cairo and to the man without whom little progress could be made towards unity. This time the Iraqis joined in the negotiations.

Nasser agreed to hold discussions in Cairo in March and April 1963. He was much more cautious this time and did not have much confidence in the Baath leaders. In talks he subjected them to severe criticism and questioned their past behaviour, which he called deceitful and opportunistic. A transcript of the talks was published and broadcast on Cairo radio. It provides a fascinating picture of the cut and thrust of argument and of how Nasser taunted the Syrians. He made it very clear that any union would be on his terms according to his new socialist precepts. Nasser's strong personality dominated the discussions and the Syrians and Iraqis tried lamely to defend themselves and to ward off his attacks. He obviously enjoyed his superiority and dominant position and his strength derived from the fact that he was still the only conceivable leader.

Although little understanding was reached over the future

political leadership or organization of the union a formal agreement was signed on 17 April with the stipulation that full implementation would have to wait for over two years. The Baathists were not fully reconciled to the idea of a union which would not allow them the free hand they sought in Syria. The internal situation remained troubled with dissension between those who supported Nasser come what may and the Baathists. Nasserist officers attempted a coup in July which the Baath led by Amin al-Hafiz bloodily put down. Some 800 people, largely innocent victims, were killed or wounded, 20 supporters of the coup were executed and hundreds more arrested. Nasser's patience was exhausted by these moves and he declared, 'We do not consider that the UAR is bound to the present fascist regime in Syria by any common aim'. The suppression of the coup left the Baath in power and General Hafiz as leader. A Sunni from Aleppo, from the lower middle class, he had risen to power with a reputation for courage and honesty. He attempted to bring together the disparate elements in Syrian political life and, while not reconciling all, he at least gave some stability to the leadership of the Baath. He remained in power from the 1963 coup until he was ousted in February 1966. The Baath Military Committee established tight control of the army; among its leading members were Salah Jadid, an able Alawi from Latakia, and Colonel Hafiz al-Asad, another Alawi who commanded the airforce. The Committee gradually infiltrated the armed forces to ensure that the most important units were under its control and to strengthen its ability to forestall any counter coups. In this process dynamic members of minority groups began to assume authority, particularly the Alawis, Druzes, Ismailis, as Sunni influence tended to diminish. This was a highly significant trend.

Another far-reaching change was in the composition of the Baath itself. Younger men began to challenge the old guard of Aflaq and Bitar, men of rural origin, often from the above minorities, with more radical socialist ideas which set them against the older middle-class elements who came largely from the towns. These younger men developed an alliance with the members of the Military Committee in opposition to the old guard. Aflaq, a visionary and no practical politician, was no match for the younger, tougher men. A man who had written that 'Nationalism is love before everything else' was ill-fitted to the rigours of political life.

The new left began to get its way. At the Syrian Regional[16]

Conference in September 1963 the leftists won a majority and began to introduce a more 'socialist' ideology, with notions such as class struggle and collective farms which provoked opposition, particularly amongst the bourgeoisie. Once again the army intervened. Bitar was sacked as prime minister and Hafiz took over with colleagues from the new Baath. Opposition to the regime continued, now of a rather different nature. The Baath government, considered by its opponents as both secular and minority-led, was denounced as atheistic and non-Arab. In April 1964 a significant event took place. Muslim Brothers and others provoked a riot in Hama against the government which responded violently by shelling the town. The unrest continued, however, and spread. Students, businessmen and others joined together and called for a return to democratic life and a freer system. Such was the discontent that Hafiz was forced to make some conciliatory gestures, bringing back Bitar for a while and relaxing some of his leftist policies. It was a losing battle, however, for the old Baath and for the opponents of the more radical policies. Syria was moving to the left and to a period of outright socialist measures. The 'regionalist' officers (those who saw Baath policies in terms of Syria) consolidated their power by dismissing many Sunni officers and bringing in Alawis and Druzes.

Aflaq saw his position and his ideas withering. In a speech to a meeting of the 'national' leadership in January 1965 he said:

> I think that this is the most cruel suffering that could befall a man
> . . . a man who is committed to principles for which he fought so
> long and for the sake of which he devoted all his life. The most
> painful suffering is when he sees such an outrageous distortion of
> his ideas and principles that he almost denies that that party was
> his party and that that movement was his movement.[17]

Aflaq resigned as secretary-general of the National Command.

The conflict continued, ostensibly between the regionalists and nationalists, that is roughly between the new Baathis of rural origin and old urban-based leadership. The former included Jadid and Asad and the latter Bitar, and now Hafiz. The struggle was over policies; it was also one of personalities and for domination of the army.

The February 1966 Coup

Matters came to a head with yet another coup, the thirteenth and the bloodiest in 17 years. It succeeded because the strong man, Hafiz al-Asad, saw his chance and deserted Amin al-Hafiz to support the coup. Amin al-Hafiz, Bitar and others of the nationalists who did not escape were imprisoned, banned from the party as traitors and Aflaq[18] and Bitar[19] later condemned to death. In practice this meant that the Baath had split – the regionalists remained in Syria, the nationalists went into exile, ending up in Baghdad. Aflaq condemned these developments as a plot to change the features of the party by some Syrian military people who had a superficial connection with the party and who were motivated by 'exclusiveness, vanity and a kind of narrowness and fanaticism'.[20]

The new men now felt free to follow new policies. Specifically they turned for support to the Soviet Union. Although not communist, Moscow gave some approval to Syria's policies and was willing to supply arms and economic aid. Equally importantly Syria and Egypt moved closer once more. Although Egypt had retained the name of the United Arab Republic it at last recognized Syrian independence. Some co-operation then ensued.

The Third Arab–Israel War 1967

Once more the course of Syrian politics was influenced by outside events over which it had little control. Since its foundation Israel had developed into a strong state militarily, continually at odds with its Arab neighbours. Both sides felt threatened by the strength of the other and the Arabs had never accepted the existence of the Jewish state. The Baath line was that Israel was an obstacle to Arab unity which had to be removed:

> The imperialist countries established Israel in order to prevent the revival of the Arabs and to hamper their unity. But the same act has been greatly instrumental in awakening our nationalist consciousness and elevating our awareness and the standard of our struggle so that we will eventually conquer both Israel and imperialism.[21]

In a speech in July 1959 Nasser had put forward his position.

If Ben Gurion or Moshe Dayan is looking for the final battle, I am now announcing here in the name of the people, the people of the United Arab Republic, that we are awaiting the final battle in order to rid ourselves of Israel's crime.

The feeling had grown in Egypt and Syria in the years to 1967 that the Arabs were capable of defeating Israel and belligerent and threatening statements were uttered. The arms race intensified and in November 1966 Egypt and Syria established a joint defence command which the Israelis saw as a threat. They feared most a united Arab stand which might lead to a simultaneous attack on three fronts (Jordan, Sinai and Syria). There were several Israeli-Syrian clashes on the border and air battles in April 1967 were followed by continuous fighting in May. The Russians warned Nasser that they had information that the Israelis had mobilized two brigades on the Syrian frontier. Kosygin, the Soviet leader, told the United Nations General Assembly after the war: 'Information started to come to the Soviet government, and I think not only us, that the Israeli government planned to strike a swift blow against Syria at the end of May with the aim of smashing it and then to transfer hostilities to the territory of the UAR.' The Israeli prime minister, Eshkol, warned that Damascus would be occupied if necessary. Nasser reacted by sending troops to the Israeli border and Syria followed suit. The claim has been made that he believed the presence of Egyptian troops would deter the Israelis from attacking Syria. It is fairly certain that the Russian information was incorrect, at least in implying that the Israelis were going to carry out more than a punitive raid. However, things had been set in motion and they acquired a momentum of their own. Israel deployed its forces. On 23 May Nasser closed the Straits of Tiran to Israeli shipping, blocking Israel's access to the Red Sea and inevitably provoking a response.

Both sides mobilized their armies and Nasser shouted, 'The Jews have threatened a war. We tell them, "You are welcome; we are ready for war".' Nevertheless, he constantly stressed that Egypt would not strike first. Even Moscow urged restraint, saying in so many words, 'You have won a political victory, now is the time to compromise'. The atmosphere in the Arab world was against compromise. King Husain of Jordan landed in Cairo on 30 May and signed a defence agreement with Egypt. Even the leader of the Palestine Liberation Organization,[22] who had earlier incited the people of Jordan to overthrow the king, sat by Husain's side. While the agreement spoke of 'repelling any attack', in public speeches Arab leaders were caught in an atmosphere of extreme threats. Damascus proclaimed that 'the elimination of Israel is essential'. Baghdad threatened 'Our goal is clear – to wipe Israel off the face of the map'.

The Israelis could not afford not to take these threats seriously. They could be defeated only once and therefore had to take pre-emptive action. Early on 5 June Israel struck. Egypt was totally defeated by 8 June, its airforce destroyed and Israeli troops once again on the Suez Canal. Jordan misguidedly joined in and immediately lost East Jerusalem and the West Bank of the Jordan which it had successfully defended in 1948/9. The Syrian and Israeli frontiers met in the Jaulan region. The way up to the Jaulan Heights 610 metres above sea level is extremely steep and was well defended on a front of only some 60 kilometres. The Syrians looked down on northern Israel from these heights and used the position to shell boats on Lake Tiberias and Israeli settlements. The Israelis were tempted by the opportunity to put an end to these attacks.

Syria had begun on 5 June by shelling towns and villages in the border area. While engaged elsewhere Israel could do little in return on the ground although it had already destroyed two-thirds of the Syrian airforce. Once Egypt and Jordan were defeated the way was open to attack Syria. Israel hesitated because of the physical difficulties and because of strong Russian support for Syria. It was unsure of the results of any attack. Would the Soviet Union intervene? The Syrians virtually ensured an Israeli attack by continuing the shelling on 8 June. By the evening when Syria had accepted a UN cease-fire resolution it was too late. The Israelis stormed up the Heights in their tanks. The Syrian army resisted fiercely but was hampered by Israeli dominance in the air. The breakthrough came because of a catastrophic misunderstanding. Early on 10 June Radio Damascus announced that Qunaitra, the chief town in the Jaulan, had fallen several hours before the Israelis arrived there. The Syrians presumably hoped that the announcement would induce the powers in the UN to impose a cease-fire on Israel before the town had fallen. It had the opposite effect. The defending Syrian troops believed that the announcement meant that they were surrounded and cut off. They therefore abandoned their positions and began to make their way back to Damascus. Later that day the Israelis entered Qunaitra without a shot being fired. The UN cease-fire came into effect at 6 p.m. and the Israeli advance halted. The loss of the area was a disaster for the Syrians and it has been a primary aim ever since to regain the territory. The Syrians also suffered severe military casualties and many civilians fled from the fighting or were later expelled by the Israelis. The occupying forces destroyed villages, cut off water supplies and threatened those inhabitants reluctant to leave the land coveted by the Israelis. Almost the only people left were the Druzes, about 5 percent of the population. No Syrians were allowed to return. On the contrary Jewish settlers were encouraged to come and establish collective farms to make the Israeli presence permanent.

The lightning and comprehensive defeat shook the Arab world and led to an attempt to analyse the reasons. The mood beforehand had been supreme confidence – afterwards astonished disbelief. How had a small state managed to defeat the combined Arab armies. Some thinkers were brave enough to suggest that the Arabs would have totally to rethink their strategy, to rebuild on a basis of realism and perhaps one day to accept Israel as an accomplished fact. In the diplomatic field the first move of the Arabs was to hold a summit conference in Khartoum in September. The leaders there were united in opposition to Israel and issued a declaration of complete rejection: no peace with Israel, no negotiations, no recognition, and the maintenance of the rights of the Palestinian people. The Arabs were to soldier on, rebuilding their armies with Soviet help in the hope that one day they would be strong enough to fight again. Certainly there would be no peace until the territories lost in the 1967 war were regained. The United Nations at least supported this latter view in Resolution 242 which stated that the acquisition of territory by war was inadmissible. It required Israel to withdraw from 'territories of recent conflict' and demanded the acknowledgement of the sovereignty of all states in the area.

The determination to carry on the fight can be viewed as a Churchillian-type refusal to contemplate defeat, or as a complete lack of realism. Like other Arab governments the Syrians insisted on calling their defeat merely a 'setback' – although Aflaq was more realistic and called it a 'national calamity' – and carried on with their uncompromising attitude. Syria refused to attend the Khartoum summit and to co-operate with 'reactionary' Arab states – Saudi Arabia and others – and opposed UN efforts to achieve a peaceful solution. The Baath leaders wanted to retain their ideological 'purity' in face of calls to compromise. In fact they met with some

opposition at home. Their opponents (Nasserists, Hawrani social-
ists and others) accused the Baath of being responsible for the
defeat and called for more democracy and less repression. The
Baathis reacted with more repression and arrests and refused to
compromise and work with others. They were themselves split in a
conflict which grew more serious because of the 1967 defeat.
Tension was caused by disputes over which military, foreign and
socio-economic policies should be pursued. The two main trends
were represented by Salah Jadid and Hafiz al-Asad, both Alawis
which made the struggle also an internal sectarian one. These two
strong personalities were rivals for supreme power. The ideological
differences centred around whether priority should be given to
doctrinaire socialist aims (Jadid) or first and foremost to Arab
co-operation in the struggle against Israel (Asad). Jadid and his
followers managed to obtain a majority for their policies at Baath
party congresses in late 1968. Asad refused to accept these decisions
and instead turned to the army in order to build up his power there.
He managed to place his supporters in many of the most influential
positions while Jadid was building his support in the civilian
apparatus. If a final clash came there could be only one result – the
army held power.

Asad also began to build up his support in the various local areas
outside Damascus. As had been mentioned, opposition in Syria
often stems from power bases outside the capital. Asad was
particularly keen to ensure his base in his home Alawi area around
Latakia. His military supporters virtually seized power there in
February 1969 and left the civilians helpless. In addition Asad's
troops took over the radio stations in Damascus and Aleppo and the
offices of the two leading newspapers in the attempt to dominate
news and propaganda.

The dual system of control between civilians and military
continued for another year until September 1970 – Black September. This was the month in which King Husain of Jordan finally
decided that the Palestinians in his country had too much power and
were in danger of taking over the running of the state themselves.
They therefore had to be crushed. This was done bloodily in
September. Syrian leaders with their commitment to Palestine felt
they could not stand idly by. On 19 September armoured units
crossed the Jordanian frontier but withdrew a few days later, having
suffered severe casualties. Perhaps surprisingly, Asad had opposed
the intervention and was strongly criticized by the civilians who had

been more reckless. This brought the split into the open. When the civilians tried to depose him, his military preparations bore fruit and he and the Chief of Staff, Mustafa Tlas, were able to take counteractions. On 13 November 1970 Asad ordered his military supporters to occupy the offices of the civilian party sections and to arrest prominent leaders including Salah Jadid and the Sunni president, Nur al-Din al-Atasi. Political power was now monopolized by officers, largely Alawi, of Asad's faction and in February 1971 he became (and has remained) the first Alawi president of Syria. This marked the final stage of the rise of the Alawis from a position of political insignificance to one of national dominance. It was the beginning of a new era in Syrian politics dominated by one man – Hafiz al-Asad.

Notes

1 P. Seale, *The struggle for Syria* (London: I. B. Tauris, 1986), p. 32.
2 The League of Arab States established by Syria and other states in 1945 to co-ordinate inter-Arab policies.
3 Seale, op. cit., p. 76.
4 ibid., p. 118. According to Seale, Zaim was almost a political gangster and Hinnawi just a puppet.
5 ibid., p. 141.
6 He went into exile in Saudi Arabia and then Brazil where he was assassinated in 1964 (ibid., p. 147).
7 M. Riad, *The struggle for peace in the Middle East* (London: Quartet, 1981), p. 9.
8 *Al-Ahram* (newspaper), 8 November 1955.
9 Baath, *Texts*, p. 1.
10 BBC, *Summary of world broadcasts* (M.E.), 688, 10 July 1956.
11 Riad, op. cit., p. 10.
12 Proclamation of the UAR, 1958.
13 Quoted in M. Kerr, *The Arab cold war*, (London: Oxford University Press, 1971), p. 45.
14 Baath, *Texts*, p. 24.
15 ibid., p. 25.
16 The Arab world in the Baath view is divided into regions, not states, awaiting reunification. Therefore it holds regional conferences, Syrian or Iraqi, and national ones which are pan-Arab.
17 Baath, *Texts*, p. 179.
18 Michel Aflaq lived in exile first in Beirut and in 1967 moved to Brazil. In 1969 he returned to Beirut in an effort to regain the leadership. He went on to Baghdad where he is an honoured guest, making frequent political statements. His slogan, 'One Arab nation with an eternal mission', decorated the buildings in Baghdad.

19 Bitar left the Syrian stage in August after he escaped from prison. He spent the rest of his life in exile, often in Baghdad where the 'rival' Baath was based. The author heard him address a conference there in 1977 when he was still passionately propagating the ideals of Arab unity as the first step towards the solution of all political problems. In Paris in July 1980 a lone assassin killed him. Was Syria responsible? A few days earlier a grenade had been thrown at President Asad and his brother had declared, 'We shall chase them [those responsible] at home and abroad'.

20 Baath, *Texts*, p. 186.

21 ibid., p. 104.

22 The Palestine Liberation Organization (PLO) was established by Palestinians in 1964 with the declared aim of carrying out armed struggle to liberate the occupied homeland.

4 *Syria under Asad 1971–1986*

> The role of extraordinary persons is undeniable in
> the making of history.   (M. Aflaq)

On 28 September 1970 Jamal Abd al-Nasser died. He had worked
himself to death. The departure of the greatest Arab leader of
modern times left a yawning gap in Arab politics. There was no
longer one leader who could dominate the scene. By a coincidence
of timing, as Nasser died Asad was beginning his tenure of power.
He became the ruler of Syria, a dominating figure but, unlike
Nasser, with little appeal to the masses outside his own country.
Hafiz al-Asad was born in Qardaha in the Latakia area of a poor
peasant Alawi family in 1928[1] in the middle of the period of the
French Mandate. Two factors helped to shape his life. As a member
of a minority he had to face decisions which do not affect members
of majorities. He could either mingle with his fellows in an attempt
to avoid discrimination or persecution, or he could break out in an
attempt to make himself successful and even indispensable in the
world of the majority. He chose the latter course and entered
the one institution which promised promotion on merit – the
army.

Growing up under the French, Asad, like many politically
minded students, did not avoid being drawn into anti-French
activities. In the 1940s his political awakening coincided with the
birth of the Baath party. Its ideas of nationalism and secularism
attracted members of minorities (its founder was after all a
Christian) who saw it as a way of gaining entrance into the
hoped-for non-sectarian national community. The Baath was only a
promise in those days and Asad joined the Homs Military Academy
in 1951 as an avenue for advancement. It is easy with hindsight to
impute qualities to young men who later make it to the top, but
Asad was a serious and clearly determined cadet who became a
combat pilot in 1954. He remained so committed to politics and

Baathi activities that during the period of the UAR he and fellow Baathi officers were transferred to Cairo where it was presumably believed they could cause less nuisance. The lesson to be learnt from exiling officers together is that they usually plot together to return and overthrow those who exiled them. Asad joined with thirteen others – mainly Alawi and Druze – in forming a Military Committee whose aims were to take Syria out of the UAR and to replace older Baath leaders who had taken Syria into union with Egypt. Three officers led the committee, Asad, Salah Jadid and Muhammad Umran. It is not clear whether one officer dominated or whether there was a struggle for leadership. In fact the split in the UAR took place while Asad was still in Egypt and he and his fellow officers returned to Syria in time to plan for the 1963 coup.

Asad's primary task on taking over in 1970 was to establish some stability in the regime. He had gained control by splitting the Baath party. He now had to gain acceptance by building up his own support and by reassuring the country that his rule was there to stay. Probably the Syrians at large welcomed the advent of the new government. The peasants and small landowners had been disappointed by the slow progress of land reform; the workers resented the austerity in the economy and the lack of improvement. All Syrians worried over the results of the 1967 war and the conduct of their leaders during it. The country sought from Asad a new start – a wider base for his regime, through more democracy and more liberal economic policies, through an attempt to legitimize his government in the eyes of the whole community and through a more relaxed approach to their Arab neighbours. Some of these hopes did begin to be realized.

Asad began to follow a more Nasserist policy and, although for the time being Syria still rejected the UN resolution 242, relations with Egypt and Jordan improved and Syria's isolation from the Arab world was reduced. In April 1971 there was even a proposal for a federation of Egypt, Libya and Syria which remained largely on paper. An impressive constitution was signed in Benghazi in Libya, largely it would seem under pressure from Colonel Qadhafi who had recently seized power in Libya. The three presidents who signed, Asad, Qadhafi and Sadat of Egypt, were all quite new in their posts and rushed into an abortive union. There is no doubt that it was a sincere, if ill thought out, attempt. The speech by the Syrian vice-president on the signing gives the flavour both of the thoughts current at the time and of Arabic rhetoric.

In Damascus, citadel of Arabism and rampart of unity, in Damascus to whose name the message of Arab unity has been tied throughout our contemporary struggle, and which realized with Cairo the first unity in the modern history of the Arabs . . . the meeting of the three presidents took place amid feelings of great support and great hopes expressed by the great Syrian people which despite all circumstances has remained faithful to Arab unity and has fought to realize it.[2]

Internally, Asad's coming to power marked a relaxation in the political atmosphere. Some political prisoners were released and he promised a restoration of civil liberties. He was elected president for a seven-year term in February 1971. A new Regional Command of the Baath was formed of Asad supporters and the old leaders were removed from their posts. A broader based People's Council was established, the first legislative body since 1966 with 173 members, of which 87 were Baathis, 8 Communists and 36 representatives of the farmers. Asad introduced what he termed a corrective regime – meaning a regime following his policies rather than those of others. One result of these policies was the centring of authority in his hands and amendments to the constitution which gave him sweeping powers.

In March 1972 further political steps were taken. The National Progressive Front – a grouping of the Baath and its allies – was set up. The eighteen-man-leadership comprised Asad, nine other Baathis and eight members of allied parties. Some legislative measures were also introduced in the economic field to encourage private enterprise and foreign investment. In the same month Syria took another significant step which is apt to be overlooked by its critics. It accepted UN Resolution 242 as a basis for a political settlement provided it really meant a full Israeli withdrawal from territories occupied in 1967 and the restitution of Palestinian rights (not fully defined). This brought Syria still closer to Egypt although Asad did not follow Sadat's lead in expelling Soviet advisers. In fact Syria and the Soviet Union became closer allies and Russia began to re-equip the Syrian forces.

The 1973 War

As Egypt and Syria were drawing closer, Jordan also was restoring links with Damascus. In the autumn of 1973 to all three countries, not to say to the whole Arab world, a solution to the conflict with Israel seemed further away than ever. The Israelis had tightened their control over the territories occupied in 1967 and had returned not one inch. In addition, East (Arab) Jerusalem had been annexed in 1967 and numerous Jewish settlements established in Sinai, the West Bank and Jaulan. Although Egypt and Jordan had expressed some willingness to negotiate, Israel had ignored all UN resolutions demanding a withdrawal. Terrorist attacks on both sides had taken place and a dangerous mood of frustration developed in the Middle East. The Arabs seemed to be making no progress in face of increasingly strong Israeli intransigence. It was believed that the USA, the strongest wholehearted supporter of Israel, was the key to progress. Certainly President Sadat was convinced that only American pressure would move Israel – pressure they appeared unwilling to exert. And the Arabs came increasingly to believe that only a new war or the threat of it would break the impasse. Secretly Syria and Egypt began to plan for war.

The attack which was launched across the Suez Canal on the morning of 6 October took outsiders by surprise. Meticulous planning and great secrecy ensured a stunning initial success. The Egyptian army quickly overran the Israeli defences on the east bank of the canal. At the same time massed Syrian armour began to advance over the 1967 ceasefire lines into the Jaulan area. Although this advance also caught the Israelis by surprise a stubborn defence and intensive air strikes stopped the Syrians before they could reach the edge of the plateau overlooking Galilee or cross the frontier into Israel proper. The Egyptians wanted the war to bring about negotiations for the return of Sinai and had no intention of crossing into Israel and threatening the civilian population. The Israelis feared that if Syria regained Jaulan it could then move into Israel and wreak havoc there. Thus it was essential to halt the Syrians and repel them, even before the Egyptians were faced and possibly thrown back across the canal.

In the end Syrian tanks were stopped just short of the old Customs House dating back to the Mandate. A few minutes more and they would have been able to cut off the road to Qunaitra and would have reached positions overlooking the steep ascent from the gorge of the Jordan. If these had been occupied the subsequent Israeli ascent up the steep and narrow road would have been much more dangerous. The Israelis by now had mobilized their reserves and men and tanks were rushed up to Jaulan. During the first week of the war the Syrian army was throwing its reserves into battle in a desperate effort to maintain its positions. The Syrians had recaptured Qunaitra and according to Israeli sources, their own 'holding operation was hanging by a thread'. Soon the Israelis had three full divisions on the ground which began inexorably to push the Syrians back. They were determined not just to hold the Syrians at the international frontier but also to occupy lost territory and even to increase the occupied area. After a day of intense artillery exchange the advance of the Israelis accelerated and by 11 October Qunaitra was back in Israeli hands and later that day the 1967 cease-fire lines were crossed and the drive down the road to Damascus begun. On 14 October they had reached a small hill near a village only 35 kilometres from the capital. By then all the ground lost in Jaulan had been retaken. The Iraqis, Jordanians and Moroccans all sent troops into the battle, to no avail. But there the advance stopped. The Israelis were then concentrating on Sinai (where they crossed the canal and trapped part of the Egyptian army) and had no desire to be drawn into a costly battle for Damascus. Syria suffered severe losses in men and equipment and from Israeli air attacks on the oil refinery at Homs, on oil terminals, power stations and other installations. Nevertheless, the Syrians felt that they had fought better than ever before and that the myth of Israeli invincibility had been dented. Asad remained defiant and, although accepting the UN cease-fire of 22 October, declared that Syria was ready to resume fighting unless Israel withdrew from Arab territory.

The war had changed attitudes, unfortunately from an Arab point of view not as much as wished. A new factor was the so-called 'oil weapon'. Some of the Arab oil producing states reduced or cut off the supply of oil to Europe and America. On 6 November the European Common Market called for an Israeli withdrawal from occupied territories in return for secure borders. Cynics could argue that Europe moved only when its pocket and own interests were threatened; in fact it had earlier begun to call for withdrawal and Resolution 242 was British sponsored. The USA, however, felt threatened by the oil shortage and the Secretary of State, Henry Kissinger, began a shuttle between Middle Eastern capitals in an attempt to work out disengagement agreements. In the winter and spring of 1974 there was danger of further war between Syria and Israel as Syria carried out a war of attrition in the Jaulan area. Syria, with Soviet support, was reluctant to come to a disengagement agreement (as Egypt had done) which did not include total Israeli withdrawal. Eventually, in May 1974 Kissinger was successful in persuading both sides to reach agreement. Israel would withdraw to the 1967 'boundaries' and evacuate a little more territory including the capital of the area, Qunaitra.

Destruction of a City

When the Syrians re-entered Qunaitra they found a scene of total devastation. The city had been fought over several times, yet it was now destroyed in a much more sinister manner. It was as though a giant fist had smashed down on most of the houses; the roofs were almost intact but level with the ground. The Israelis on withdrawing had systematically blown up the houses. A UN official reported that he watched from a distance as the Israeli troops dynamited the houses while the UN force waited to move in after withdrawal. Two eyewitnesses reported on their visits to Qunaitra soon after the Israeli withdrawal. They both confirmed the senseless destruction.

> On all sides the scenery was horribly familiar; bulldozed heaps of masonry, half-uprooted trees, cracked and snapped concrete roofs . . . The hospital remains but pocked and raked with bullet holes and with its window frames ripped out and electrical fittings removed. It is horribly mutilated . . . the sight of row after row of levelled and mutilated houses is a considerable horror to witness but . . . as we slowly approached one of the city's cemeteries . . . we experienced something far worse . . . In the majority of cases the square iron doors of the tombs had been forced open and the coffin lids removed.[3]

The graves had been looted.

The blow to Syria was enormous. It served to increase the determination not to compromise any more, not to consider any peace agreement until all Jaulan was restored and the Palestinians' rights recognized. It strengthened the hands of those who preached steadfastness in the face of Israeli occupation and the resolve, if necessary, to go it alone without the help of Arab allies. Qunaitra remains uninhabited and cut off from its surrounding agricultural hinterland. During the following year Syria attempted unsuccessfully to secure further Israeli withdrawal. The Americans had appeared for a time to be a little more co-operative when President

Nixon visited Damascus in June 1974. His welcome was less effusive than that he received in Cairo but there did seem to be some relaxation in relations between the USA and Syria. It did not last long. Syria was suspicious of moves to secure a further disengagement between Egypt and Israel while the Israelis refused to budge in Jaulan. Asad saw the Israeli-Egyptian agreement signed in September 1975 as an unforgivable breach in Arab solidarity. He angrily attacked Sadat whom he believed to be a traitor to the Arab cause. His compromise with Israel had 'been one of buying land and rewarding the aggressor with billions of dollars in return for a few kilometres of land. This will push Israel towards more arrogance, upholding the occupation of the land . . . We are struggling for the achievement of a just peace in the area.'[4] This attitude of complete refusal to compromise Arab ideals isolated Syria in the struggle against Israel. It felt both that it had been unfairly left to continue the fight alone and that Sadat had compromised at the expense both of Syria and the Palestinians. The quarrel with Iraq became equally bitter. Once again Asad felt betrayed when Iraqi troops had been abruptly withdrawn 24 hours after Syria had reluctantly accepted the cease-fire in October 1973. Iraq attacked Syria for its apparent acceptance of a peaceful solution, hurling abuse from a safe distance.

It is not clear that the Syrians themselves had been consistently unremitting in the struggle. Some claimed that in October 1973 elements of the Syrian army had been withdrawn from the front to defend the regime in Damascus rather than fight the enemy. Asad's position was not totally secure and rumour circulated about rivalry within the Alawi community itself, particularly between Hafiz al-Asad and his flamboyant brother Rifaat. (This rivalry continued at least until 1984.) Just before the Sixth Syrian Regional Congress of the Baath party, hundreds of members were arrested in a purge of opponents but significantly during the same congress Rifaat was elected a member of the Syrian Regional Command next to his brother.

War in Lebanon

Once again it was events outside Syria which were to have far reaching effects on its internal and external policies. Lebanon was to draw Syria into an apparently endless involvement. The concept of Greater Syria has been mentioned several times and it is firmly believed in the Arab world that the natural unity of the area was destroyed when Britain and France carved it up into four separate entities in 1920. Despite this *de facto* division Syria has nevertheless had a particular interest in Lebanon and felt a responsibility for developments there.

In Lebanon itself things went from bad to worse. Since its foundation the country had tried to exist on a consensus between its Muslim and Christian inhabitants, who were divided into roughly equal portions. It was the only country in the Arab world with such a large percentage of Christians, where there was a Christian president and where they dominated much of the trade and banking. For a time the consensus worked fairly well and Lebanon prospered. Two trends disturbed the situation. The number of Palestinian refugees in the country had grown and they were beginning to behave as though they were a state within a state particularly in the south. Then the Muslims, notably the Shiis who had been the poorest and most underprivileged section, began to resent both the Christians' claims to dominance and their own secondary status. In 1975 a number of incidents led to outbreaks of fighting and quickly the country plunged into civil war, although there were so many armed groups and factions it was not always clear which was fighting which. The Syrians were alarmed by the instability on their borders and were anxious to avert a situation which might tempt Israel to interfere. Asad decided that intervention was necessary in order to prevent further deterioration and in June 1976 Syrian troops crossed into Lebanon, ostensibly to support the Christians against a section of the Palestinians. They were soon drawn into the struggle and later switched sides on more than one occasion. They were enmeshed in the bewildering maelstrom of Lebanese politics.[5] The fundamental motive of Syrian policy was the belief in the indivisibility of the two countries. Asad claimed that 'Throughout history Syria and Lebanon have been one country and people'.[6] There was never a Syrian embassy in Beirut and from time to time there was an open frontier. The president also said, 'It is difficult to draw a line between Lebanese security in the broad sense and Syria's security' but added, 'We ask nothing of Lebanon and have no ambitions there'.[7] The first stage of the fighting in Lebanon ended with a cease-fire in October. Other Arab states deeply mistrusted Syrian motives but the Syrians agreed to withdraw only if their troops were replaced by an adequate Arab

League force. This was in fact accepted and in mid-November an Arab deterrent force entered Beirut with soldiers from several Arab states although Syria still provided the overwhelming majority.[8]

President Asad's prestige was considerably raised by the ending of the fighting but the maintenance of troops in Lebanon caused severe financial strain. Although the richer Arab oil states helped with finance, states such as Saudi Arabia, conservative and traditional, did not welcome the extension of Syrian influence and the looming possibility of a greater Syria coming into being – or at least of Lebanon remaining under permanent Syrian domination. Asad himself was worried by the possibility of provoking Israeli reaction if Syrian troops moved too far south in Lebanon towards the Israeli frontier. The Palestinians in southern Lebanon were running their own mini-state and when in March 1978 Israel invaded the area in an attempt to clear it of Palestinian guerrillas and Syria was unable to intervene, Asad saw it as a threat to all Arabs. 'We must bear in mind that one of the principal objectives of Israel's invasion of the Lebanon is to reduce the Arab nation to despair and make the Arab masses believe that Israel is strong and capable of achieving what it wants, so that it is useless to resist its aggression.'[9]

Yet another traumatic event was in the making in November 1977 when President Sadat of Egypt travelled to Jerusalem to meet Israeli leaders and actually to address the Knesset (parliament). Arab opinion was stunned by this effrontery. Asad was furious at this further betrayal and joined with other states in a front of steadfastness directed against Egyptian compromise. The Syrians declared, 'We will not attend any conference in the presence of Sadat'. The Egyptian president retorted, 'The attitude of Syria . . . is one of hatred, bitterness, inability and ignorance'. For a time this quarrel drew Syria and Iraq closer together as Israel, Egypt and the USA met for talks at Camp David in September 1978. Asad visited Baghdad in October and the two Baath parties agreed to bury their differences. The euphoria of *rapprochement* led to another attempt at Arab unity. In 1979 moves were announced towards union between Iraq and Syria. With their common Baathi ideology the two states agreed to set up committees to study the project. But rivalry and suspicion proved stronger than brotherhood and all the talks and goodwill came to nothing. The two leaders, Asad of Syria and Saddam Husain of Iraq, mistrusted each other. The two wings of the Baath were led by very different groupings – the Alawis in

Syria and the Tikritis (a Sunni clan) in Iraq. In August there was an attempted coup against Saddam, and Asad was immediately suspected. That put an end to unity and the feuding recommenced.

In Syria itself a plebiscite in February 1978 had confirmed Asad as president with a large majority for a second seven-year term of office. No one doubted that he would be re-elected. However, this did not mean that there was no opposition within the country to the government he led. Unrest was growing for which there was a number of causes. The traditional rivalry among the different cities and areas of the country continued and this was intensified by opposition to the Alawi predominance in the government. In addition the Muslim Brothers stepped up their activities. They objected both to the Alawis about whose Islamic orthodoxy they had great doubt and to the avowedly secularist policy of the Baath party. The initial policy in Lebanon by which Syrians seemed to be fighting against Muslims and the PLO added to the anti-Alawi feeling. Finally, the depressed state of the economy deepened the opposition. Assassinations of Alawis became an increasing problem. The opposition showed extraordinary confidence when in June 1979 gunmen made their way into the Aleppo artillery school and massacred over 60 cadets, mostly Alawi. This daring probably proved that the Ikhwan had infiltrated the army. Asad reacted quickly, rounding up several hundred alleged members of the Ikhwan and other government critics. A number of them was executed that summer. There was rioting in Latakia in September which was also anti-Alawi where it is claimed more than forty Alawis were killed. Such violence caused a severe reaction on the part of the government which felt that its whole position was being threatened. At first Asad was cautious in his moves, unwilling to unleash a chain of action and reaction. He brought new members to the party leadership, replaced other officials including the prime minister and promised a greater degree of rule by law.

The opposition did not reciprocate and took to the streets, especially in Aleppo. In March 1980 several different sections of the opposition came together in a series of strikes, demonstrations and riots. Parts of the city were virtually out of control. The merchants declared a general strike which spread to other towns. Some groups of professions, lawyers, academics and others rather bravely made demands for more democracy and the release of political prisoners. There was a feeling that all the disturbances were directed against the Alawis. Asad had to react and 12,000 troops under the command of his brother were sent to Aleppo to isolate the city. Such a challenge to authority could not remain ignored. Unfortunately the opposition was not cowed and resisted the troops. It is reported that hundreds were killed in the fighting – the exact number is unknown. Many activist opponents were arrested and imprisoned. In Paris in July 1980 an assassin killed Salah al-Din Bitar, who represented Syrian opposition forces in Iraq and had just published a series of newspaper articles analysing the Syrian regime. Syria was accused of the killing. Rifaat al-Asad had said: 'We shall chase them [opponents] at home and abroad . . . We are prepared to exterminate a million citizens in order to ensure safety and defend the revolution.' Five days earlier a grenade had been thrown at Hafiz al-Asad. This was followed by the execution of several hundred political prisoners in Palmyra. It was reported that up to 300 members of the regime were assassinated by dissidents and an explosion in the prime minister's house killed 20 people. The government blamed outside agents for the unrest – Iraq, Israel and the USA. While it is not unlikely that Iraq encouraged opposition, there were nevertheless deep internal grievances, particularly among the Sunni Muslims; cassettes were circulated containing anti-regime sermons; prayers in houses were used as a cover for political meetings; and there was more veiling among women – an obvious and silent sign of protest. The government had to be careful not to offend all Muslim opinion and tried to draw a distinction between the ordinary devout believer who would not espouse violence and those members of the Ikhwan who were willing to commit murder. Asad declared: 'We encourage anybody who works for religion and to uphold religious values.'[10]

Once again, however, external events conspired to disturb the course of Syrian politics. The Syrian army was still committed in Lebanon when in September 1980 war broke out between Iraq and Iran. Syrian antagonism towards Iraq was so strong that Asad surprisingly moved to support the non-Arab side in the war – Khomeini's Iran. The official Syrian justification was: 'We support Iran because it is anti-Israeli as the Shah was not. We have a pact of unity with Iraq. Let Iraq announce its commitment to this pact and the war will stop immediately because Iran cannot fight Syria and Iraq combined.'[11] Mustafa Tlas added more colourfully: 'Saddam Husain – this pipsqueak still dreams of conquering Iran and doesn't know that the Americans will never allow him to be strong enough to do it.'[12]

This led to a total break with Iraq. It also caused difficulties with Jordan which actively backed its Arab neighbour Iraq in the war. Syria felt isolated and accused both Jordan and Iraq of supporting the Ikhwan against it. Asad also suspected King Husain's move towards President Reagan and the USA as he saw it as another step in possible negotiations with Israel which would bypass Syria. The personal attacks between Husain and Asad became very bitter. For a time the two armies faced each other menacingly across the frontier but instability would have helped neither regime and the two sides drew back from conflict.

In Lebanon Syrian troops were engaged in fighting Christian forces in the Bekaa valley east of the mountains. Israel felt impelled to intervene and its aircraft made repeated flights over Lebanon. Two Syrian helicopters were shot down and the Syrians moved missiles into the valley to try to deter further Israeli attacks. Immediately Israel threatened to knock them out and a prolonged crisis ensued with the two countries on the brink of war. Eventually, with Saudi and Kuwaiti mediation, the Christian forces agreed to withdraw and for a few months the crisis was eased.

Annexation

The next blow to fall on Syria was an Israeli move which was certain to incense all Syrians, supporters of Asad or not. Jaulan, occupied in June 1967, was finally annexed by Israel in December 1981. This was intolerable and hardened Syrian determination not to compromise. Syria felt betrayed by Egypt which was slowly getting back *its* occupied land in Sinai. After the occupation of Jaulan in 1967 Israel's first action had been to expel about 100,000 Syrians excluding the Druze population which Israel, despite great opposition, tried to woo by reasonable treatment. Druzes were offered Israeli citizenship and this was followed by a campaign to force identity cards on them. By July 1981 it was estimated that only some 400 had accepted. A Druze leaflet stated, 'We are against the occupation. The Jaulan Heights are part of Arab Syria.' In December the Israeli prime minister, Menachem Begin, a firm believer in Israeli expansion, rushed through the law of annexation. The Druzes resisted by refusing to take Israeli citizenship. Four religious leaders were arrested and 13,000 Druzes went on strike, closing shops, schools and factories. In reaction in April Israeli troops moved into the villages, imposed a curfew and delivered Israeli identity cards. Those who refused to open their doors had their windows broken and the cards were thrown in. They were simply thrown back at the soldiers who withdrew to shouts of 'We are Syrians'. They left the streets littered with discarded identity cards. Nevertheless, the annexation has continued and its return to Syria would be an absolute condition of any peace process.

Syria's embarrassment abroad did nothing to stem the opposition at home. In fact, the situation worsened. The most serious events occurred in Hama. The Hama area had long been a centre of opposition to the government and of strong religious feeling. Certain economic changes had upset the traditional relations between smaller traders and artisans, the peasants and new industrial workers. The traders felt aggrieved and were ripe for revolt. Their discontent combined with Islamic resentment provided the spark. In February 1982 serious fighting broke out between Hama residents and the Syrian army. The troops had been raiding buildings in which some Ikhwan were believed to be in hiding when they were attacked by Ikhwan using guns and grenades. The fighting soon spread and was fanned by a call from the mosques for a general uprising. Public buildings were looted and set on fire and many Baath members and their families killed. The Iraqis interfered by allowing a broadcast to be made from their territory urging a 'civil mutiny' against the Syrian regime.

The government reaction was extreme as it felt that its whole position was threatened. Some 12,000 troops with tanks, artillery and helicopters were engaged in heavy actions which totally destroyed parts of the city. It is said that many thousands of civilians were killed although exact figures are not available. The 'Command of the Islamic Revolution' in Syria (the Ikhwan) issued several reports on the fighting. To them the army's activities were brutal and merciless and the resistance of their fighters (*mujahidin*) heroic. They were fighting in the name of Islam. As one report stated: 'The people of Hama have risen in arms . . . How has it happened? It was the only choice – the only choice to save the nation.'[13] One Syrian soldier is reported to have said: 'I saw the doors and windows of the houses opened and the people shouted "*Allahu akbar* [God is the greatest]. Go away, murderers, we want Islam". The loud-speakers of the mosque were used to call people to wage *jihad* [war] against us.'[14]

The result of the use of overwhelming force against lightly armed opponents was inevitable. The regime saw compromise as weakness and was ruthless in its actions. Hama was battered into submission and the rising did not spread to other cities. The army stayed loyal to the regime (apart from the alleged defection of one brigade) and the Ikhwan did not gain any widespread support. Asad blamed them (and Iraq and America!) for the rising and claimed that true Muslims did not oppose him. 'They [the Ikhwan] carried out every act banned by God . . . They are apostates. We are the ones who defend Islam, religion and the homeland.'

The events in Hama had as a consequence the formal establish-ment of a broad opposition grouping, named the National Alliance for the Liberation of Syria. It issued a declaration in March 1982 which called for 'the use of all possible means, especially armed public struggle to topple the present dictatorial regime'. The fight would be shared by all parties and people as long as they were not anti-Islamic. Asad was criticized for dividing Lebanon into small sectarian states, for crushing the PLO and for handing over Jaulan to the enemy! He was equally castigated for attacks on Islamic values.[15]

The Baathi government feeling threatened and isolated, lashed out at those it felt responsible for its situation. In March it issued a communiqué calling on the Iraqi masses to liberate their country from 'terror and treason' by overthrowing the 'fascist puppet regime'. Almost the only friend of Syria was Iran, ironically the revolutionary Islamic state befriending a government considered non-Islamic by its Muslim opponents. A joint Syro-Iranian state-ment condemned Iraq for starting the war and agreements between the two states led to economic co-operation.

Asad's government was somehow riding the storm, determined not to compromise with deeply held principles – even in isolation and under threat. Syria was helpless when faced with the next disaster – the Israeli invasion of Lebanon in June 1982. This was code-named 'Peace for Galilee' and was ostensibly an attempt to put an end to Palestinian raids across the Israeli border from south Lebanon. The real reason was to eradicate completely the PLO presence in Lebanon. Much more was involved as the invasion led to a confrontation with Syria. On 8 June the Syrians and Israelis fought a massive air battle over Beirut which the Israelis won decisively and left them in control of the air above the city. The next day they attacked the Syrian missile sites in the Bekaa valley and reportedly destroyed seventeen. Once again the Syrians faced an all-out war which they did not feel able to win. Thus they evacuated Beirut and the Israeli forces quickly reached the city, trapping the PLO there. The Israelis pounded the city for many days and laid siege to it, cutting off supplies and access. By late August the PLO was forced to leave the city for various ports in the Mediterranean. The Israelis did not enter the city and eventually withdrew to the south.

Despite the Israeli intervention in Lebanon Syria remained the one outside power which was able in any way to influence the course of events. Lebanese leaders looked to Damascus for guidance and took their plans for the future there for approval. This did not mean that Syria was able (or willing) to impose a solution militarily. That would have needed an enormous military effort and expenditure. It did mean that a solution unacceptable to Syria was unlikely to succeed. Syria was willing to try to maintain a balance among the various competing factions by not allowing any one to become too strong. An official Syrian spokesman declared: 'The Lebanese should know that we do not covet a single speck of Lebanese soil. To speak of Syrian domination of the Lebanese government is nonsense and an utter fabrication. Our strategy stands on the basis of no victor, no vanquished.'[16] However, Syria did want to dominate the PLO to ensure that it did not make any moves towards a settlement with Israel which would leave Syria even more isolated. This eventually meant that when the PLO leader, Yasir Arafat, began to show signs of a willingness to talk, Syria backed a breakaway Palestinian faction which supported its rejectionist stand.

Syria was able to demonstrate some influence in May 1983 when Israel and Lebanon came to an agreement which formally ended the state of war between the two countries which had lasted since 1948. Israel agreed to withdraw from Lebanon in return for the recognition of a security area in the south which would be jointly supervised by the two states. This area would preserve the security of northern Israel and would stretch from the Mediterranean to Jaulan. The Americans, who had helped to negotiate the agreement, expressed their understanding that the Israeli withdrawal would take place only if Syria also agreed to withdraw. Asad totally refused to co-operate. He argued that Israel would retain a privileged position in an Arab country and that Syria's special relationship with Lebanon was being ignored. And so the agreement – much hailed as a breakthrough – remained a dead letter. Asad stated: 'We approve of whatever security measures the Lebanese government of national reconciliation is prepared to take so long as these are measures taken by the Lebanese armed forces alone. There can be no Israeli soldiers on Lebanese soil.'[17] The agreement was abrogated in March 1984.

The Americans had underestimated Syrian determination. More Syrian missiles had been deployed in Lebanon and the Syrian forces equipped by the Soviet Union considerably strengthened. The Americans in addition made sure of a Syrian refusal by taking the Lebanese-Israeli agreement to Damascus as a *fait accompli* without having bothered to consult the Syrians beforehand. Syria's policy was defined as: 'Our strategy requires the continuation of the war against Israel; we have to go on combating it and join with it in all-out battle. Continued wars with Israel mould the spirit of revolution among the Arab people.'[18]

In fact the Syrian position was somewhat stronger as their ability to wreck agreements made without them had demonstrated. They continued to support various factions in the endless Lebanese fighting and were not adverse to switching sides if it were considered politic. Thus in November 1983 Syria decided to bring to a head the split in the PLO when Arafat and his supporters were trapped in Tripoli in northern Lebanon. Syrian troops and PLO rebels fought fiercely against him and he and some 4000 followers were eventually forced to leave the city in December under United Nations protection. Syria had not gained control of the PLO but Arafat's position was considerably weakened within the movement. This led him to appear more moderate and to be moving towards a possible accommodation with Jordan, which could have led to negotiations with Israel.

Syria declared its total opposition to such negotiations; if they started: 'We would overturn the table. We cannot let any individual hijack what is the decision of the people. Our concern is not to allow anyone to proceed alone with any solution at the expense of the cause as a whole.'[19] They were equally dismissive of Arafat who was believed to have sold out to the USA. As Tlas explained picturesquely:

The case with the PLO was the following: after the withdrawal from Beirut Arafat thought he could depend totally on the Americans . . . When the theatrical thunder died down in Tripoli Don Quixote-Arafat withdrew from the front under the protection of the US 6th fleet with the help of the French and with the tacit permission of Israel. The PLO must cleanse its ranks of traitors. Arafat has catapulted himself out of the PLO. No Palestinian should suffer the illusion that Palestine could be freed without the participation of Syria.[20]

The split between the Syrian-backed faction of the PLO and Arafat's wing widened. In December 1984 the Palestine National Council (the parliament in exile) met in Amman and decided to turn away from Syrian militancy towards Jordanian moderation. The fact that the PNC met in Jordan in the face of Syrian opposition was significant. The Syrian faction was too weak to stand alone and the majority even supported Arafat's visit to Cairo to try to mend fences with President Mubarak. This move tended to isolate Syria the more and it announced the formation of a front dedicated to the overthrow of the Jordanian government. In December a leading member of the PLO Executive was assassinated in Amman and Arafat immediately accused Syria of being behind the murder. He also claimed that there was a Syrian campaign against other pro-Arafat Palestinians. The Syrians denied this and replied that it was all a plot hatched by Arafat, Jordan, USA and Israel! 'They wheel and deal in the name of the Palestinian national decision while negotiating with the enemies of the Palestine people . . . Syria will not be pushed into the wings. Its concern is to reject the capitulationist solution.'[21]

Internally in Syria there were interesting developments. It was reported in November 1983 that President Asad was ill, supposedly as the result of a heart attack although this was denied by the Syrian authorities. Asad's position was so central to stability that Syria held its breath until he recovered. He dominates the scene and his disappearance could lead to widespread disturbances and possible army intervention. He is not an international figure as was Nasser or Sadat but his presence and authority have had to be reckoned with on the national and international scene. He has suppressed opposition so ruthlessly that he has created many enemies although younger Syrians have known nothing but Baathi rule and Asad and are often prepared to keep out of politics. Urban Sunnis look upon the Alawis as country people but ask whether Asad has really been so bad. Would an alternative be worse? He has brought stability, he stands up to Israel and the USA and has promoted some development in the country. His brother Rifaat, a possible successor, is looked upon as corrupt and excessive in his life style and in the use of his special forces, the Defence Companies, especially in Hama. He is criticized for favouring the USA where he sent his sons to be educated. He built a large house nicknamed the palazzo near Washington which was promptly burned down (by Israeli agents it is said).

When Hafiz was ill Rifaat flooded Syria with posters of himself, smiling and looking heavenwards. When Hafiz recovered, Syria breathed a sigh of relief and the police tore the posters down. Nevertheless, Rifaat demanded changes in the army command and when Hafiz refused he brought his troops on to the streets of Damascus near the presidential palace. Hafiz brought in regular troops commanded by his brother-in-law and for some days the two forces faced each other at opposite ends of the street. Hafiz arrested one of Rifaat's senior commanders in the Defence Companies and the opposition soon collapsed. The Baath party met in urgent sessions and decided to make Rifaat one of three vice-presidents. Mustafa Tlas was still there as Minister of Defence where the real power lay. The political situation was precarious, however, and this open Alawi quarrelling did not improve the image of the regime.

As Asad retook control the tension in Syria eased. Rifaat was sent off to Moscow in a delegation in May and not allowed home. (Tlas declared him *persona non grata* and said that anyone who said no to Asad would be a head shorter.) Hafiz used his absence to weaken his brother's centres of power. The Defence Companies were reduced in number – from 60–70,000 to 15–18,000 – and were integrated into the army. The University Graduates Association, which Rifaat used as a political vehicle in opposition to the Baath, was closed down and his smuggling activities stamped on. He was allowed to return to Damascus in November with his power severely curtailed. His position and other problems were discussed at the Eighth Congress of the Syrian Baath party. No firm decision seemed to have been made on the problem of the succession to Hafiz and although Rifaat retained his seat on the Central Committee he was given no chance to speak or explain himself. Hafiz's position was strengthened when the congress passed, as expected, a vote of confidence in his continued leadership. In elections to the presidency in February 1985 Asad was re-elected for a further term of office with a reported 99.97 per cent of the votes cast – he was the only candidate. The congress had openly discussed the country's other problems – shortage of consumer goods, the socialist running of the country and corruption.

In the field of foreign relations the real success had been Syria's ability to dismantle the Israeli-Lebanese agreement. Factional fighting continued in Lebanon and the Israelis came under severe attack from Shii fighters in the south. They finally had to withdraw in June 1985 but retained the right to police a buffer zone in the south with the co-operation of the South Lebanon army. At least Syria had gained a partial success which appeared to be reinforced when the warring parties signed a cease-fire in October and a peace agreement in December. Unfortunately this soon broke down and fighting continued throughout 1986. Some shifts in alliances took place and late in the year the Shii militia were fighting the Palestinians who had returned to the south of Lebanon. Israel was once again attacking suspected PLO concentrations in the areas they had supposedly cleared.

1986 was not an easy year for Syria. In an attempt to ease his isolation Asad held talks with King Husain of Jordan after the period of hostility. Despite their differing attitudes towards the PLO (with Syria backing the anti-Arafat faction) Husain at least admitted that 'Jordanian minority groups [Muslim brothers]' had 'undertaken destructive activities in Syria' and that these would henceforth cease. They both declared themselves against 'partial, separate and direct talks with Israel' and agreed that any settlement should take place at a general peace conference. Husain also tried to bring Syria and Iraq together again – with no success. Iraq could not forgive Syria's support of Iran in the continuing war between the two countries. Asad seemed to want to lessen his isolation in the Arab world, particularly as opposition to the regime was manifest once more. A large car bomb exploded in Damascus in March and there were numerous explosions on buses and trains in April. Many civilians were reported to have been killed.

International Relations

Syria's relations with the outside world have been described in part. At the forefront are its relations with other Arab states, although strictly speaking according to Baath ideology the Arab world is one and therefore relations among Arab states are internal. This does not mean that the relationship is easy; it has often been marked by disputes and quarrels. Syria's absolute adherence to its ideology has led to isolation and to strange allies, notably Iran. The alliance with the Soviet Union has been essential to Syria's development. Such an alliance is not easy as it is not between equals. Although Syria has had to depend on Russia for the supply of military equipment and for aid in various forms, it has no wish to become a client or satellite state. Having thrown off French rule, Syria wanted no further tutelage from a great power. The partnership was not to be one of domination or dictation. Nor could there be any question, as happened in Eastern Europe, of Russia imposing its own ideology on weaker states. Russia as one of the two superpowers conducts its policy in competition with the United States. Apart from areas where the supremacy of the other is recognized, Russia demands the right to participate in world affairs on equal terms. The Middle East in the Soviet view should not be an American preserve. The Soviet fleet has full access to the Mediterranean and its ports, Russia claims a part in any negotiations over the future of the Palestinians and supports one side or the other in internal or international disputes. The Soviet Union suffers two disadvantages in comparison with the USA and Europe. First, the kinds of goods and technology it can supply are sometimes inferior to those of the West or are unsuitable, and secondly, as communist parties are mostly banned in the Arab world, relationships are sometimes strained and the Soviet Union finds itself aiding regimes it considers bourgeois or even anti-communist.

The Soviet Union entered the Middle Eastern scene in a significant manner when Nasser announced an agreement to purchase Czech (Russian) arms in September 1955. He had despaired of obtaining weapons unconditionally from Britain or the USA and turned to the Soviet bloc. This move influenced Syria and a Soviet trade and financial agreement was signed in November 1955 and in 1956 Czech arms began to arrive. At the same time the Communist Party in Syria was making some progress. The best known Arab communist, Khalid Bakdash, Secretary General of the SCP, had been elected to parliament in 1954. He often visited Russia and spoke at CPSU congresses. He was never able, however, to play a very large role in the government of Syria.

Soviet commentators on the whole approved of Syrian politics at the time even though they were not full-blown socialist. The government was bourgeois with a clear, progressive anti-imperialist line and it was hoped that in the future it would join the socialist camp. After the breakup of the United Arab Republic in 1961 Khrushchev, the Soviet leader, said that he hoped that the USSR would develop 'business-like co-operation' with Syria, but the coup of 1963 brought to power the Baath party which was distrusted both by the Russians and the Syrian communists. Bakdash characterized the Baathis as 'a band of adventurers, spies and saboteurs isolated from the people, who undermine the Arab liberation movement'.[22] The Russians have learned by experience that they cannot avoid relations with governments whose policies they dislike and they slowly came to accept the Syrian Baath. Their criticism of Baath ideology lessened and they noted that in 1964 under Amin al-Hafiz more acceptable socialist policies were being introduced. A *rapprochement* between Moscow and Damascus began when Syrian economic and military delegations visited the Russian capital later in 1964. When Bitar and Aflaq left the front of the stage Soviet commentators considered the new leaders to be less reactionary than the former bourgeois middle class and more committed to socialism. Syria was now looked upon as a progressive regime preparing to build socialism.

This meant that relations became closer and in April 1966 the Soviet Union expressed its willingness to help to build the new dam on the Euphrates river. (This is a mirror of Soviet aid in building the Aswan Dam in Egypt.) Moscow said it looked upon Syria as a neighbour which meant that it could not remain indifferent to Western or Israeli attempts to encroach on Syria's rights. When the Syrian and Israeli airforces clashed in April 1967 and severe losses were inflicted on the Syrians flying Russian planes, the Russians were furious at what they called Israeli 'aggression' and warned that it was 'dangerous playing with fire on the part of Israel in an area near the borders of the Soviet Union'.[23] After the 1967 war Soviet support for Syria increased and the arms lost were replaced with newer and better versions. The lesson of the war from the Russian point of view was that 'Only unity on an anti-imperialist basis, the development of democracy and radical social change, friendship with the Soviet Union and other socialist countries can frustrate the imperialist plot against the Arab states'.[24]

The struggle for leadership within the Baath between Asad and his opponents posed another problem for the Russians. At first the struggle was ignored and then, when faced with the *fait accompli* of Asad taking over, Moscow realized it had to co-operate with the new leaders. The Soviets gradually came round to full approval and welcomed Asad on his visit to Moscow in February 1971 when he came to ask for economic and military assistance. The two sides drew closer and in addition to material support (a $700 million arms deal was reported) the Kremlin promised to help to eliminate the 'Israeli aggression'. The Baath party itself was classified by Soviet commentators as revolutionary and progressive and in the vanguard of the anti-imperialist struggle.

Advanced Soviet military equipment was sent to Syria together with thousands of advisers. These moves raised the tension with Israel which tried to restore the balance by destroying Syrian aircraft in air battles. The numbers of Russian SAM missiles were increased in order to try to counter these Israeli air attacks. At the beginning of the 1973 war Syrian missiles were able to inflict damage on the Israeli airforce until they were gradually overwhelmed by massive retaliatory air strikes. After the loss of several hundred tanks and numerous missiles the Soviet Union agreed to restock the Syrian forces. The Russians were now fully committed to defending Syrian integrity and were being drawn into the conflict. They demanded a cease-fire on 22 October at the UN and warned Israel of serious consequences if it were not observed. When Israel continued to fight, Moscow threatened to send in its own troops, either jointly with US forces or through unilateral action. Washington reacted by declaring a state of military alert. It is far from certain that the Soviet Union really intended to intervene or was capable of sending large-scale troop contingents to the area. The threat was more likely calculated to cause an American response in exerting pressure on Israel to observe the cease-fire. This worked and both Syria and Egypt were saved from further Israeli hostilities.

Immediately after the war Syria established a direct relationship with the USA, Kissinger, the American Secretary of State, using his shuttle diplomacy in an attempt to put an end to the Syrian-Israeli confrontation. A disengagement agreement was signed in May 1974 and Syria recognized the American role in achieving this. There seemed to be an attempt to avoid an exclusive reliance on only one super-power but by 1978/9 Washington became increasingly suspect as it helped in the exclusive Egyptian-Israeli peace process. The USA was now the enemy plotting to dominate the Middle East and contacts between the two virtually ceased. Syria no longer expected the USA to play any positive role in promoting a Middle East peace settlement and therefore adopted its hard line and pro-Soviet position. Asad denounced Washington as the 'arch enemy' of the Arab people.

Moscow was portrayed as the friend of the Arabs, willing to back Syria in its struggle against Israel. Asad visited Moscow in October 1979 to make further requests for arms deliveries. This close relationship was sealed by the signing in October 1980 of a Treaty of Friendship and Co-operation. It had been preceded by a number of exchange visits and the Baath Party Congress in August had given its formal sanction. Asad, concerned over criticism of the treaty, made an effort to assure other Arab states that it did not mean subordination to Moscow nor, presumably, a negation of Islamic values. He wanted both to stress that he was still his own man and to reassure countries such as Saudi Arabia (aid-giver to Syria) and his own Muslims that an alliance with an atheist state did not mean any commitment to its values. It followed the pattern of other Soviet treaties and included promises of military co-operation and consultation in the event of a threat to the peace or security of either side. In 1986 Syria became the Soviet Union's largest Third World purchaser of arms. Deliveries included helicopters, patrol boats, missiles, tanks and submarines. There were reported to be some 5,000 East European and Soviet military advisers in Syria and Soviet military ships have access to Syrian ports.

The Syrian-Soviet relationship has been close if uneasy. The policies of the two countries do not always coincide. For example, to Syrian annoyance Moscow continued to support Arafat and his wing of the PLO, and to lean towards the Baathi regime in Iraq which also has a Treaty of Friendship with Russia. Asad visited Moscow in November 1984 and despite Secretary Chernenko's assurances of 'full support and all-round assistance' there were reports of coolness between the two leaders. Chernenko called for an international Middle Eastern peace conference involving Russia and the PLO, a call not echoed by Asad who merely called the proposals 'realistic'. Mustafa Tlas neatly summed up the relationship: 'President Asad is a very proud man whom nobody can push around. The Russians understand that . . . These talks were always between equal partners and not between a super-power and a vassal . . . The USA views [King Husain and President Mubarak] as vassals.'[25]

The United States have found Asad's Syria a difficult state to deal with. The American categorization of Syria has trapped them into an unyielding position. Syria is portrayed as a Soviet client, the sponsor of terrorism, regional mischief maker and the implacable foe of US and Israeli interests. According to a former US ambassador to Damascus, the 'hyperbole, bombast and sloganeering of the Syrian media' do not help the Syrian negative image in the United States. According to Mustafa Tlas: 'As long as the Americans scorn us and treat us without dignity I won't give a damn about America.'[26] Relations improved for a time when Asad was seen to have helped secure the release of American hostages in the hijacked plane in Beirut in June 1985. President Reagan publicly thanked him and Syria's role in a future Middle East settlement was recognized. The American president even assured him that he wanted an Israel withdrawal from Jaulan. This lasted for a time only, as the Americans quickly reverted to accusing Syria of international terrorist activities. When Libya was bombed in April 1986 it was assumed that the real, but too dangerous a target was Syria. The sentencing of Nizar Hindawi for attempting to blow up an Israeli airliner brought these accusations into the open. He was convicted as a Syrian agent and diplomatic relations between Britain and Syria were suspended. Other countries took less drastic actions. Syria vehemently denied being involved in terrorism and any deliberate worsening of its international reputation would seem to be counter-productive. Syria certainly would not invite Israel's retaliation at a time when it is absorbing new Soviet arms and is not prepared for war. It could have been a deliberate move by the Syrian opposition to weaken Asad's position or an independent plan of the Syrian secret services unknown to Asad. Many accusations and counter-claims flew back and forth but there seemed to be no good reason for the usually cautious Asad to expose himself to international opprobium.

Notes

1 Sources disagree over the year of his birth – 1928, 1929, 1930, 1931?
2 *Texte du Communiqué* . . . 20 août 1971.
3 'The destruction of Kunaitra', by Lawrence Grey, *Middle East International*, November 1974, p. 24.
4 BBC, *Summary of world broadcasts* (M.E.), 17 September 1975.
5 12 years later they were still there in a situation still unsolved.
6 BBC, loc. cit., 22 July 1976.
7 ibid., 28 June 1975.
8 Since then most non-Syrians have dropped out.

5 Politics and Ideologies

The Baath view has opened a new path in thinking
and feeling.   (M. Aflaq)

Arab Nationalism

The concept of Arab nationalism has been at the root of Syrian
politics and its banner has been carried by the Syrians more
devotedly than by any other group of Arabs. Arab nationalism –
that sense of solidarity among those having a language, culture and
(largely) a religion in common – developed during the early part of
this century under the influence of, and as a reaction against,
European nationalism. It was expressed as the desire of the Arabs
to live in an independent state, which would include all Arabs,
however defined, although more specifically in the beginning the
Arabs of Greater Syria, Arabia and Iraq.

It is based on the strong belief that there is an Arab nation, that it
should form a single independent unit to the benefit of all its
members. This feeling was strongest among Ottoman Syrians and
when an Arab (National) Congress was held in Paris in 1913 the
large majority of members was Syrian-Muslim and Christian. At the
same time secret Arab societies were formed which called for
complete independence from the Ottoman Empire. During the
First World War many Arabs joined the fight against the Turks in
the hope that they would gain independence if the Ottomans were
defeated. With their hopes shattered by the imposition of the
Mandates and the splitting of Syria/Arabia into several states, the
ideal of Arab nationalism was now expressed in first gaining
independence from Britain and France and then moving towards
unity. Syrian politicians continued to adhere to the concept of
Greater Syria as the essential part of a larger Arab unity.

After gaining independence in 1945 the new Syrian government
declared that 'The Arab alliance is an accomplished fact and the
great Arab state will be realized'. Although this was an expression
of hope rather than reality it was nevertheless an affirmation of

deeply held convictions. When the United Arab Republic was
proclaimed thirteen years later the joint Syrian-Egyptian proclamation stated:

> Unity should be established between the two countries as a
> preliminary step towards the realization of complete Arab
> unity . . . Arab nationalism has been the inspiring spirit dominat-
> ing the history of the Arabs in all their different countries, their
> common present and the hoped-for future of every Arab . . .
> Arab nationalism is the Arabs' path to sovereignty and freedom.[1]

Although the UAR failed, other attempts at unity have been
made and Syria's commitment to the ideal is unwavering. Its
resistance to a separate peace with Israel or to anything less than
complete Palestinian independence has been in the name of Arab
solidarity. In a speech in August 1985 to the Syrian armed forces
Asad underlined his commitment to Arab nationalism:

> The army . . . has now become a source of pride for the people
> and the nation; a pride that is mixed with a strong belief in the
> unity of the Arab Nation, the unity of its destiny . . . While we
> see Arab regimes around us racing along the road to capitulation,
> Syria should double its efforts to prevent total Arab collapse.
> [Those Arab rulers who followed the path of] capitulation . . .
> have ignored the broad interests of their Arab peoples and
> Nation and have preferred to achieve their little and personal
> interests.[2]

Politics before Baathism: National Bloc

Before the adoption of Baathism as the official ideology of the state
in 1963 politics in Syria had followed no fixed path. A number of
movements or parties had arisen often without clear ideologies and
in many cases with no firm organization. The course of politics in the
interwar period had been distorted by the presence of the French
and an independent political life had had very little chance to
develop. There was no previous experience of parliament or party
and everything had to be learned by trial or error. Political
groupings were often formed on the basis of personal relationships
or local loyalties rather than ideological conviction.

The first recognizable grouping was the National Bloc formed in 1928 from elected members of the National Assembly. It was a working alliance of professionals, intellectuals, notables (whose wealth was largely based on land-ownership) and large merchants. They led a group of lesser notables, small merchants and traders and members of the bourgeoisie. Influence was based on long-lived loyalties and on personalities who traditionally had local prestige. It was not an ideologically based political party, rather a modification of earlier patterns of authority. Its programme was vague, calling for complete independence for all Arab countries, and its most important move was the drawing up of the first Syrian constitution. It was basically a European democratic constitution[3] promising free elections, equality for all before the law and religious freedom. It was rejected by the French.

After the Second World War the veteran politicians began to lose influence and the National Bloc split in two, largely on the basis of personalities and local loyalties. Quwatli, Mardam and others from Damascus formed the National Party; the People's Party was mainly an Aleppo party together with Atasi from Homs. There were no real differences in their policies and they were largely interested in holding on to their position. They retained some semblance of power even after the army had first intervened and in 1950 under President Shishakli, the former colonel, the old politicians in the National Assembly drew up a new constitution. The aspiration of the Syrian people was expressed in the preamble.

> We proclaim that our people, which is part of the Arab nation by its history, its present and future, wishes for the day when once again our Arab nation will be reunited in a single state.

Syria was to be a democratic parliamentary republic in which all people were equal and individual freedom was guaranteed. It was another liberal, parliamentary constitution, somewhat ironically drawn up under a military regime. Two of its clauses stipulated that the president had to be a Muslim and that Islamic law (*sharia*) was the principal source of legislation. Many of its provisions were overtaken by events. It was a late attempt by the old nationalists to put Syria on the path to a liberal democracy. Their powers were, however, gradually weakened by their infighting and irrelevance, and by the growth of the power of the army and the Baath party. Younger men were taking over with their own very firm ideas.

Syrian National Party

In the 1930s there developed a number of political parties which tried to appeal to the young and to introduce a tighter organization. The Syrian National Party was founded by a Lebanese Christian brought up in Brazil, Antun Saada, who became the 'leader'. It was strictly organized as a totalitarian party with total allegiance to the leader whose word was law. Its membership gradually grew until it was claimed to have 50,000 members, some of whom formed a militia. In 1949 Saada was involved in a plot in Lebanon, captured, tried and executed. The party's influence was strongest there although it had sympathizers in Syria. Its ideology was that a Syrian nation existed in geographical Syria but that there was no Arab nation. There were Arab peoples of which Syrians were one. The party stressed national loyalty above all and believed that its mission was to create a powerful all-consuming national life. In this the SNP resembled the fascist parties of Europe. It was exclusively secular in character and this stemmed logically from the founder being a Christian living in a Muslim majority.

In April 1955 the SNP faced a terminal crisis. In that month the deputy chief of staff of the Syrian army, Adnan Malki, was shot dead by a disgruntled military police sergeant. The motives of the assassin were a mix of the personal and political and the crime caused political turmoil in Syria. He was identified as a member of the SNP and the party was thought at the time to be attempting to gain control of the army in opposition to the Baath. The reaction was extreme and many members of the SNP were accused of plotting revolt, murder and treason. The SNP was itself accused of being a secret society incompatible with Syrian political life. The Communists (rivals of the SNP) joined with the Baath in clamouring for its elimination, and on all sides it was condemned. Antun Saada's widow was sentenced to imprisonment and other leaders convicted in their absence. This spelt the end of the SNP in Syrian political life.

Arab Socialist Party

Akram Hawrani was a young activist figure from Hama, anxious to participate in direct political action, who had tried to assassinate the Syrian president in 1932. He joined the SNP for a while and then founded his own Youth Party, in reaction to the methods and authority of the National Bloc. He wanted more urgent action and was an impatient young man. He was elected to parliament in 1943 as member for Hama. In 1945 he organized his own Arab Socialist Party which, clearly in opposition to the landowning members of the National Bloc, called for the elimination of feudalism, the distribution of land to the landless and other radical policies. The ASP proclaimed the slogans of socialism and Arab unity.

He was an energetic leader and built up a substantial following among the young in the army and the peasants in the neighbourhood of Hama who rejected the feudal and poverty-stricken conditions under which they had to live. He represented new, young, radical forces in Syria which resented the power of the older nationalists. In 1952, in opposition to the other political forces in Syria, Hawrani united his Arab Socialist Party with the Baath and together they were to change the course of Syrian politics.

Muslim Brotherhood

Another notable development was the foundation of the Muslim Brotherhood – *Ikhwan al-Muslimin* – in Egypt in 1928. They represented the age-old trend in Islamic history which believed that all difficulties in Islamic society originated in a deviation from the ideals of early Islam. Their founder was Hasan al-Banna, a gifted religious leader with talents both as preacher and organizer. The aims of the Ikhwan were elaborated by al-Banna to his followers as:

> You are not a benevolent society, nor a political party, nor a local association having limited purposes. Rather, you are a new spirit making its way into the heart of this nation to give it life by means of the Quran . . . When asked what it is you propagate, reply that it is Islam, the message of Muhammad, the religion that contains within it government. If you are told that you are political, answer that Islam admits no such distinction.[4]

Islam to the Ikhwan was a total system containing within itself everything necessary for life in contemporary society. They had firm attitudes towards politics, the economy, education, culture and the role of women. The Ikhwan grew as a movement in Egypt where it was deeply involved in the struggle against the British. Its ideas were universally attractive to the Islamic community and soon spread to Syria. It began in Aleppo and Damascus under different guises until 1945 when the term Ikhwan was adopted. The aim of the movement in Syria was to unite all Arabs and Muslims, not just those of Syria and Lebanon. It was a 'world movement which represented a new resurrection amongst Arab and Muslim youths'.

The Ikhwan began to play a role in Syrian politics, following an Islamic line amongst the conflicting personal and ideological trends. They had an uneven career. In 1949 they formed an Islamic Socialist Front to stand in elections and advertized their opposition to reforms they considered secular or under foreign influence. In 1952 in an effort to quell opposition to their activities, Shishakli's government ordered the dissolution of the Ikhwan and the closure of their offices and schools. In the 1954 elections they could not, therefore, contest seats and backed those candidates they considered 'good Muslims'. Their political message was unaltered – Muslim solidarity and opposition to the West. They also preached opposition to Nasser's regime in Egypt which was waging a bitter struggle against the Ikhwan. (In October 1954 Nasser narrowly escaped assassination by a member of the Ikhwan.)

The ideas of the Ikhwan in Syria remained attractive to certain sections of the population, although their role in politics diminished as the Baath rose to power and during the UAR (1958–61) they remained completely banned. They rose to spectacular prominence some fifteen years later.

Communism

At the other end of the political spectrum from an organization aiming to build society on the basis of religion is the one dedicated to the abolition of religion and the establishment of scientific socialism. The Syrian Communist Party was founded in 1930 and led in 1934 by, among others, Khalid Bakdash, a young Kurdish law student from Damascus. Under him in the 1930s the party followed a policy of demanding first of all national independence, leaving aside more revolutionary demands. Disputes broke out between the SCP snd the National Bloc which led to the SCP's suppression in 1939. The Communists had criticized the Bloc for not restricting the privileges of the feudal landowners and had claimed that national re-birth would be brought about only by the people. Most of the

Communist leaders were arrested and only released in 1941 when the British and Free French occupied Syria. The Communists were then back in favour as Russia was allied with Britain and France in the war against Germany. The party stressed friendly ties with the Soviet Union and continued to work for national independence. After the war the earlier rivalry reappeared and when Russia blotted its copybook in 1947 by voting in favour of a Jewish state in Palestine, anti-Communist demonstrations took place in Damascus and the party was again suppressed and its leaders arrested. It remained illegal from 1948 until the fall of Shishakli in 1954 when Communists took part in the September elections. Their leader, Bakdash, was elected for Damascus – the first Communist to become a member of an Arab parliament. Although he was alone, he was a capable leader and able to organize the party into an efficient, if small, body. Its support stemmed largely from the professional classes, less so from the urban proletariat and hardly at all from the peasants. It was not strong enough to assume power itself and the Baath had a much stronger following in the army and among students. Some form of co-operation seemed advisable and as the Baath moved to the left an alliance was made in 1957.

During the period of the United Arab Republic all political parties, other than the officially sponsored Egyptian National Union, were banned. The Communists refused to be banned and the members left the country or were jailed. After the break-up of the union they were kept in jail until 1962 and Bakdash remained in exile (he did not return until 1986). Once the Baath and the army came to power the Communists were condemned to a subsidiary role. Asad allowed them to participate in politics as representatives of progressive parties although he was criticized for this by other Arab leaders who were imprisoning or executing their own Communists. While the Soviet Union plays a large role in Syria's life the Communists can expect a quiet time as long as they are content with their very subsidiary role. Asad stresses that 'Our Party is not a Marxist party. It is a socialist party with nationalist leanings.'[5]

The Baath Party

The ideology of the Baath party was to have (and continues to have) a profound influence on Syrian politics. The ideology was compre-

hensively and exclusively Arab; its slogan 'One Arab nation with an
eternal message'. An understanding of Baath ideas is essential for
an understanding of contemporary Syria and they are best expressed in the words of the two founders of the party, Michel Aflaq and
Salah al-Din Bitar.[6] They came from a traditional background in
Damascus 'which strongly maintained time-honoured traditions,
which were permeated with certain values of Arab chivalry [but] we
were not traditionalists . . . we were rebels and revolutionaries. We
came from the people and shared their misfortunes.' In Syria
between 1924 and 1930 young students were concerned with
agitation against the French Mandate authorities. 'From an early
age we were in the battle.'

It was in Paris, where we were studying at the Sorbonne 1930–34,
that we gave vent to our Arab consciousness. We were in
permanent contact with other Arab students . . . This naturally
led us to discuss the struggles for national liberation, but also
freedom and socialism.

They returned to Syria in 1934 to find the country

seething with excitement . . . We were already armed with
progressive social and even socialist but still essentially Arab
ideas. They necessarily distinguished us from Syrian communists
who espoused internationalism . . . Our indifference to, and
then separation from, the traditional political movement represented by the National Bloc Party and our progress toward the
creation of a modern revolutionary movement dates from that
time.

'The year 1939 may be considered as the actual year of the birth of
the Baath.' After the Second World War had ended and Syria had
gained independence 'the mood favoured the transformation of the
movement into a party'. The first Baath Party Congress was held in
April 1946 and the main principles of Baathism then laid down.
    Arab nationalism is the core of Baath ideology, but the concept is
a romantic, almost mystical, one far removed from the rough and
tumble of everyday politics. The Baath should be a

humane, historic movement which would satisfy all aspirations
and the thirst for values and ideals in the Arab spirit . . . [It

should] restore the connection between our present and our glorious past . . . the past for which we long . . . Fundamentally the Baath is more than a party. It is a state of mind, an atmosphere, a faith, a doctrine, a culture, a civilization with its own worth. Arabism is at the centre of the Baathist doctrine and is the core of its doctrine of unshakeable faith in the creative genius of a nation with a glorious and noble past . . . It is the awakening of instinct, of intelligence and of consciousness, reflecting a desire for one's own recognition, for affirmation in the eyes of others, and for the recovery by the Arabs of their national existence in the world.

The only solution to the Arab problem is unity. The Arab world is artifically divided and Baathis always refer to it as the 'Arab people in the different parts of its homeland'. 'Unity is not something automatic . . . it is a fundamental and living idea, an ideal and a standard, a struggle which should come from the innermost depths of the masses.' 'Arab unity will not be reached in one stroke, but it is natural and reasonable that it should be achieved in stages.'

Freedom will come to the Arabs only with unity. 'What liberty could be wider and greater than binding oneself to the renaissance of one's nation and its revolution?' 'The liberty we seek is not opposed to legislative measures to curb exploitation by feudalists, capitalists and opportunists. It is a new and strict liberty which stands against pressure and confusion.' 'Dictatorship is a precarious, unsuitable and self-contradictory system which does not allow the consciousness of the people to grow.'

An essential part of Baath ideology is socialism, a benevolent and humane socialism. 'Unity must be accompanied by a social revolution which brings equality and prosperity. Socialism would be an increase in the wealth of life . . . and every individual should be allowed to realize his gifts and potential . . . allowing every Arab without distinction or discrimination to become a tangibly productive entity.' 'Man is the supreme value . . . while capitalism is the reverse.' Later, in the 1960s, Aflaq moved closer to a Marxist interpretation of socialism: 'Marxism is a socialist theory, but we must look at it objectively. Our stand today against Marxism and Communism is no longer negative . . . we must take what is of benefit to us in our socialist struggle.' 'We are part of the working class' which really means the nation.

Baathism as an Arab movement sprang from Arab history and

therefore was deeply indebted to Islam and Muhammad, the prophet who enshrined Arab history. 'Every Arab at present can live the life of the Arab prophet.' 'Muhammad concentrated all his efforts to produce the Arab nation.' 'Muhammad was all the Arabs. Let all Arabs of today be Muhammad.' As a Christian, Aflaq had to acknowledge the essential role of Islam in Arabism, yet he could not admit that to be an Arab one had to be a Muslim. He had to portray Islam as almost an extra-religious component of Arab nationalism and this has led to condemnation of Baathism as a secular movement and of Aflaq as an atheist. His retort was: 'The connection of Islam to Arabism is not similar to that of any religion to any nationalism. The Arab Christians when [Arab] nationalism is fully awakened . . . will recognize that for them Islam is nationalist education. Islam is the most precious thing in their Arabism.' 'Religion is fundamental in the life of humanity but we have to differentiate between religion with its true and genuine aims and religion as incorporated in certain concepts, conventions, customs, and interests.' 'We do not approve of atheism . . . [it] is a false attitude. Revolution against religion in Europe is itself a religion. It is a belief in high human ideals.' To Aflaq, nationalism was his religion.

From the above brief summary it is clear that the Baathism of Aflaq and Bitar was a liberal and idealistic doctrine. Although Bitar did hold political office, Aflaq was the visionary, the dreamer rather unfitted for political life. Their ideas were appropriated by younger less idealistic military men who were to rule in the name of Baathism but in a way which eventually alienated the two founders. Aflaq had said in 1957: 'What we want to say about the function of the army is that the military should not be involved in the tasks of leadership of the party or the government.' The cut and thrust of politics was not for him: 'Machiavellism which resorts to lying and gives no regard to ethics should never be applied.' Bitar saw the hijacking of their movement as a 'heavy blow [against] progressive forces. A hardening of the Baath ensued . . . [with] authoritarianism and intellectual and moral terrorism which would necessarily lead to liquidations within the party and to a total break from the popular masses. Marginal currents sprang up in the party and . . . an opportunist movement . . . sought to take into its own hands the leadership and the machinery of the party. They were young officers without any experience or political horizon, so-called leftists . . . puffed up with political ambition [they] wanted to finish both with the Arab ideology of the party and with its founders.' On 25 February 1966 'a military putsch overthrew the leadership of the party of which I [Bitar] was a member as well as the government of which I was the head. The "regionalists" took over, by force of arms, the leadership . . . That was the end of the Baath. In its place a new construction was erected, fully equipped and pre-eminently leftish. A neo-Baath came into being and [the original] – the movement of Arab renaissance – was put to death.' Aflaq no longer recognized the Baath party as his; it was an 'outrageous distortion' of his ideas and principles.

Both men were expelled from Syrian politics. Bitar announced in 1968 that he would break away from all Baathi wrangling as 'these parties had ceased to be what they set out to be, retaining only their names and acting as the organs of power and the instruments of regional and dictatorial regimes'. He was assassinated in 1980, most likely because of his outspokenness in criticizing the Syrian regime. In Iraq, Aflaq continued to propagate slightly modified views. After the 1967 war which he saw as a 'national calamity' he declared: 'We need the whole Arab people to be a recruited army – in this way we can release all the latent powers of our people.' The 1973 war bore within it signs of the hoped-for future in the Arab world: 'It released tremendous and creative forces and potential [and was] the consequence of a profound interaction between the souls of the Arab people. [This is] an ethical force. It is heroism . . . a comprehension of the destiny of man.' In 1942 Aflaq had said: 'Our ideology is the optimistic spirit which is confident in itself, its nation and the future.' In 1974 he said: 'Steadfastness and optimism are required now.' After thirty-two years of the problems and struggles of the Middle East there is something rather splendid in the man who can remain optimistic. Aflaq continued as the ideologue of Baathism, although in terms of political power he remained on the sidelines.

Baath in Power

The Baath came to power in the wake of the military coup of March 1963, not through the ballot box as Aflaq and Bitar had presupposed. Although the ideology of the new army men was Baathism it was not the founders of the party who were in charge. Nominally, Bitar was prime minister for a time. It was the National Revolutionary Command Council of military officers which held power. Thus the character of Baathism changed. The older politicians lost out and younger, more radical men took over. The period 1963 to 1970 when Asad finally succeeded was marked ideologically by uncertainty and even turbulence. It was a period of transition from the old nationalist politicians to the radical socialist Baathis.

There are several features of the period which can be singled out. There was a gradual change of support for the leaders of the government from the original backing of the peasants and workers to a more bourgeois base of middle and larger merchants; the move of the minorities, particularly the Alawis, to the centre of power in the army; the struggle between the army and the Baath party; and finally the constant underlining of the Baath ideology as all other political opponents were silenced. Contradictions were still evident in the period. While Baathism is based on unity, there were growing splits – between Syria and Iraq, Syria and Egypt, between moderates and radicals, between Sunnis and Alawis, and among the Alawis themselves. It was as though Baathism was an umbrella under which all those sheltering quarrelled among themselves. Even the secretariat of the Baath Military Bureau was moved to criticize this factionalism. Writing in 1965 it said:

> The highest party leaders were isolated from supervising and directing the organization because at first they were confronting the difficult circumstances of the revolution. Afterwards they became submerged in authority affairs, as well as in a fierce struggle for power, which created weakness of discipline and education in the Party, and subsequently [led to] a lack and loss of unity in thought, spirit and orientation. This caused the organization to end up in a state of mutilation which the comrades could not tolerate. Thus party loyalty was replaced by loyalty to a person or bloc.[7]

The struggle between 'moderates' and radicals was centred on the dispute whether to impose a radical left wing government and a social revolution on Syria or to follow a more moderate Arab-unionist course which would possibly appease opponents of the Baath. The radicals largely held the upper hand and worked to strengthen the control of the party over the state. The struggle for ultimate control of the party and army intensified during a period of intensive political manoeuvring.

Despite these splits a Provisional Constitution[8] was approved in April 1964 which firmly restated Baathi principles.

The Arab people of Syria are part of the Arab nation, they believe in unity and work toward its achievement; sovereignty in the region belongs to the people; the state is interested in the growth of a generation strong in body, mind and character with faith in its spiritual heritage and pride in its Arab virtues.

According to this constitution the state assumes feelings and interests in the population (e.g. 'The state shall protect and encourage marriage'), becomes all-caring and all-seeing. The people can no longer express their views in elections as neither they nor a parliament are provided for. All powers, legislative and executive, reside in the National Revolutionary Council which is not elected but consists of 'its present membership and representatives of the people'. How new members are to be chosen is left unstated. The NRC is to elect its president and also the Executive Council which is to be the active ministerial cabinet of the government. The NRC was charged with holding a public plebiscite, the purpose of which was not stated. Great stress was laid on the socialist nature and aims of the new regime: 'Natural resources are the property of the people; the socialist society is based on collective ownership of the means of production.' State ownership would be the norm although private ownership and property were not prohibited.

In the realm of actual politics the major development occurred with the February 1966 coup. The split was partly over ideology – the move to the left by the new Baath – and partly over personalities and allegiances with Asad, Jadid and their fellow Alawis ousting Sunnis and Christians. In 1966 military mobilization proved decisive and the moderates were ousted because they were seen as a threat to the revolutionary vision of the new leaders. The moderates were overrepresented by Sunni and urban elements and their departure enhanced the position of the minorities at the centre of the new Baath. From then on the Baath was split between the 'regionalists' who ruled in Syria and the 'nationalists' who fled to Baghdad. The new leaders set out to establish their position and that of the new Baath in the face of strong opposition from the old establishment. The new political system began to take shape, with its tripartite arrangement, the party, the bureaucracy and the

military. The radical drive led to attempts to challenge other more
traditional Arab regimes and Western interests in the Middle East.
However, there were still personal and even sectarian rivalries
within the Baath and the 1967 defeat undermined faith in the
radical push. Tension increased in disputes over which military,
foreign and socio-economic policies should be followed. Asad
supported the trend which suggested that the revolution be held in
abeyance in favour of Arab co-operation against Israel. Jadid
supported the opposite trend. Asad outmanoeuvred his opponents
and the radicals fell from power. It was a personal battle in which
Asad came out on top; it was also the failure of the radicals to gain
support for their policies.

Asad and the Baath 1970–

Asad has continued to rule in the name of the Baath party while
consolidating his personal power. In this third Baathi phase he has
largely abandoned the effort to accelerate the radical revolution in
Syria and has attempted instead to consolidate the Baath government, to widen support for the regime and to strengthen the armed
forces *vis-à-vis* Israel – all in the effort to gain legitimacy for his rule
and government. He had inherited a party which retained a certain
legitimacy but he had not been elected by the people at large. If he
were not to remain absolute dictator, he had to attempt to win
acceptance among the population. He decided to emphasize his
own leadership while relying on immediate support from his Alawi
relations and colleagues. He sought to eliminate the past factionalism in the Baath and make good the lack of an institutional
apparatus in Syria.

In personalizing his presidency (in the manner of Nasser) he was
raised noticeably above the other members of the government and
ruling élite in party and army. This led to a certain cult of
personality and Asad, like other powerful leaders, is not averse to
having inordinate praise heaped upon him. The Minister of Culture
obliged thus in 1985:

President Hafiz al-Asad [has a] comprehensive culture, [an]
experience of struggle, [an] experience of politics in peace and
war, [a] lively intelligence, all of which fitted him to be instigator
of the blessed corrective movement of 1970 and the hero of our

people and nation in the war of liberation of October 1973, and to be its wise leader, courageous in the armed struggle for the victory which no obstacle, neither hardship, sacrifice nor length of time, can render impossible for us or for him.[9]

He has had to build up his power on non-institutional bases which might collapse at any time – his net of Alawi supporters in strategic positions in the army, with a number of regiments loyal to him personally, and an alliance with Sunni officers and Baath officials. As the Sunnis form the overwhelming proportion of the population he cannot afford to alienate them and he has tried to bring urban Sunnis into the party leadership. He has also tried to appeal to the middle-class professionals who may be Baath members or members of progressive non-Baathi organizations. Asad, although relying on Alawi support, has had to try to play a balancing role between factions and, as has been shown earlier, while still retaining power personally he has not always been successful. Opposition has been regional and sectarian, personal and ideological, and has been dealt with ruthlessly, through wrongful imprisonment, torture, kidnapping and assassination. His power base at the centre seems to be stable but has he established institutionalized organs which will eventually ensure a peaceful transition to a new leader?

How Asad Rules

Most leaders who have strengthened their own positions wish to establish certain organizations through which the people may publicly express their support. Under the Baath party, regional congresses are held at which delegates debate government policy and on occasions go further than merely rubber stamping. At the Eighth Congress held in January 1985, 771 delegates were present. The most prominent were members of Asad's inner circle known as the *jamaa* – the group – which is Syria's political élite. The others were party members from the army, the security services, the professions and universities, the rural middle class, together with workers and peasants. The delegates debated, often in small committees, for fourteen days and elected members of the higher party bodies, the Central Committee, and the Regional Command which is the executive organ of the party headed by the president and responsible for supervising the activities of the government.

The elections were pre-arranged with the candidates nominated by
the ruling élite who thus ensured renewal of their own power. They
were then able to control the course of the debate and stifle any real
criticism. The congress is a time for Asad and his circle to meet party
delegates in an attempt to shape policy. In this way he decides how
the party's powers are exercised while at the same time appearing
receptive to the view of the general party members. Congresses
offer them the opportunity to appear to take part in the process of
government and give the president the chance to assess the mood of
his loyal supporters. The regime does encourage debate of certain
issues affecting the economy and domestic affairs as a way of testing
the feasibility and popularity of future policies. The debate cannot
go too far and this is recognized by both sides. Once a policy is
decided upon the government ends debate and enforces its decisions.

The institution of the People's Council gives a further tinge of
democracy and parliamentarianism to the system. It consists of
elected members who sit for four years, of whom half are peasants
and workers. Its activities in theory are wide, in practice limited. It
nominates the presidential candidates, discusses government policy, enacts laws and approves the budget. It could, again in theory,
force the Council of Ministers to resign although brave would be the
deputies who forced through a motion of no confidence. To add to
the parliamentary aura, members of officially approved parties
other than the Baath may stand for election. In the election of
February 1986 the Baath won 129 seats, the National Progressive
Front (mainly socialist) 57, and the Communists 9.

Mobilization

Most one party non-parliamentary regimes retain a similar state
structure – or at least aspire to it. The party is the political vanguard,
the army the agency for ensuring compliance and non-opposition,
and the bureaucracy the executive arm.

The party, more or less ideologically motivated, is the means of
inspiring loyalty to the regime and of spearheading revolutionary
changes in society. Baath leaders saw that power could not be
secured and the revolution carried through unless acceptance of
their aims was felt throughout society. To achieve this and to ensure
contact between top and bottom, the Baath has set up a series of

organizations which are aimed at mobilizing specific sections of the population – e.g. peasants, youth, women. In addition the party needs active members who will propagate party doctrine, run local and national bureaus, and oversee and inspire the larger organizations. It is estimated that there are some 100,000 active party members in Syria and that about one third of the population has been brought into the mass organizations, most of them from the lower-middle and lower classes and particularly from the rural areas. There thus remain many people outside party ranks.

The Baath has faced numerous problems of organization, problems by no means unique to Syria. Rapid modernization needs large numbers of trained leaders and these are hard to come by. Old members have been ousted, younger ones brought in sometimes on the basis of kinship, clientage or friendship and not on the basis of commitment or expertise. Often party membership is seen merely as a means of promotion. These faults have not gone unnoticed and have been criticized in party documents. Other problems are caused by the local and sectarian divisions of Syrian society and by the positions of the traditional leaders loath to surrender authority. Tradition is always struggling against modernization. Nevertheless, the party has made progress in establishing itself, in mobilizing public opinion in its favour and in acting as a means of communication in transmitting both political and technological ideas. The party is both a means of control, of limiting opposition, and of indoctrination. By cutting across sect, class and region it helps to keep Syrian society together, particularly in the villages. In towns the loyalties of the masses are more uncertain as the activities of the Ikhwan demonstrate.

Party cadres are recruited from the community, especially educated young men who form the local leadership, and from peasants who are members of the peasant unions. Syrian political life was already strong at the local level and the Baath had been active in the countryside before taking power at the centre. Consequently some party activists were already available locally, others have had to be trained in special party schools. Once trained they are sent back to their villages and towns to organize the basic party structures and to act as intermediaries between the central party and the masses. In this way the party attempts to gain the support and confidence of the people. The system works well if the local leaders are committed to the aims of the party and if the local people accept their leadership. If not, the system may break down;

the cadres may use their office for personal ambitions or be at heart still a traditional type of leader not fully committed to the Baath's modernizing policies. The local people themselves have to be convinced of the value of new policies, otherwise they will accept them superficially and pursue them half-heartedly, if at all. The central leadership is aware of actual or potential problems and urges local activists to intensify their efforts to mobilize the population. At the Baath Regional Congress of 1980 the shortcomings of party organization were made all too clear. They included 'inadequate ideological education, indifference, lack of party spirit, opportunism and an inherited devotion to sectarianism and regionalism'.

The Army

Every non-elected regime has to rely ultimately on its armed forces to remain in power. The state maintains its authority through the military and security organizations. As the army grows stronger opposition to the regime becomes more dangerous and bloody. Asad's government is prepared to use military muscle to quell opposition. The loyalty of the army, of paramount importance, he has tried to ensure by promoting Baathi and often Alawi officers. The paramilitary defence regiments have been run by Asad's brother, but ironically have also for a time been a source of opposition. Alawi favouritism has irritated Sunni and non-Baathi officers and to combat this Asad has given them greater responsibilities while retaining Alawi loyalists in key positions. The army has a privileged position in society and the greater its stake in the status quo the less likely it is to turn against the regime. It has also to believe in the cause it is fighting for. Loyalty to the homeland has to be supplemented by a conviction in its aims.

The Bureaucracy

A modern state places enormous demands on its bureaucracy, particularly in a centralized administration and economy. It is the bureaucrats who try to put into practice the numerous plans and directives which emanate from the centre. An efficient bureaucracy also helps to consolidate the party in the country at large. Syria has had to recruit large numbers of bureaucrats who, as they owe their livelihood to the state, are usually loyal and compliant, but as in all developing countries the need for skilled, motivated administrators always outstrips supply. This leads to inefficiency and to an unwillingness to take the initiative – the chief fault of many minor bureaucrats in the Middle East. At present the Syrian bureaucracy, although not a source of opposition to the regime, is not yet the efficient instrument necessary for the modernization of the country.

Alawis and Power

The significant change brought about by the Baath after 1966 in Syrian politics has been the prominent role of Alawi leaders. The Alawis were traditionally poor peasants from the Latakia region, far from the centres of urban power in the hands of the Sunni families, and suffered persecution as members of a suspect minority sect. Two ways out of the situation were open to them; the army where the French discriminated in favour of minorities and where they could escape from their poverty and seek promotion; and the Baath party with its socialism and secularism. Consequently the minorities were overrepresented in army and party in proportion to their overall numbers in the country.

A minority often tries to remain inconspicuous in order to avoid persecution. A minority leadership of a country must both play down its exclusivity and try to bring in members of other groups. The Alawis have attempted to keep a low profile while at the same time relying on intra-Alawi relationships to retain their position. They have occupied a number of key positions in government and army and at one time formed almost a quarter of the Revolutionary Command Council, the Sunnis less than one half. Asad remedied this situation by increasing the representation of Sunnis in the RCC to three-quarters. The prime minister has always been a Sunni. The increase in Sunni representation was not, however, at the expense of the Alawis but of other minorities.

The obvious colouring of the regime does lay it open to charges of sectarianism. When Asad rapped Sadat for his visit to Israel, the Egyptian president replied in kind by calling the Syrian regime 'firstly Alawi, secondly Baathi and thirdly Syrian'. Those who suffered in the Syrian Regional Command from not being of the right sect complained 'The weapon of sectarianism . . . is the ugliest and most despicable thing that could be directed not only at the struggle of the Party . . . but at the struggle of the entire Arab nation.'[10]

Sunni Muslim opposition is easily aroused by the secularist nature of Baathism and whatever Asad tries to do, the two most prominent figures in the regime, he and his brother, are Alawi – and Sunnis tend to exaggerate the Alawi nature of the regime. It is this perception of reality rather than the reality itself which can foment discontent. This unrest and exaggeration may obscure the regime's aims of introducing socialism and of cementing the nation together. Asad only gains legitimacy when the regime is recognized as acting on behalf of the whole country, both Sunni middle classes and Alawi poor. His reliance on Alawi support is necessary as long as he feels insecure or threatened and it is in his long-term interest to try to widen the basis of his support as much as possible.

Politics and Islam

Asad's position as an Alawi ruling a Sunni majority has been complicated by the fact that throughout the Islamic world there has recently been a stirring of religious feeling. Many Muslims have felt that their societies have deteriorated, due to a falling off in religious observance. Sometimes this feeling has been focused into opposition against leaders and regimes which have been blamed for a decline in Islamic devotion. The Shah's government in Iran was overturned because of its pro-Western and non-Islamic stance; President Sadat was assassinated in Egypt for 'disobeying the ordinances of God'. In Syria the opposition movement has been mentioned and there has been the series of uprisings against the regime. The Muslim Brothers and their militant colleagues, the Freedom Fighters in Syria, who together form the Islamic Front have led the opposition. They publish a journal in which their ideas are very clearly laid out. The root of their opposition stems from their view that the Baathi regime is 'dictatorial and repressive' with 'sectarian practices' 'which harm the interest of Syria, the Arabs and the Muslims and constitute grave treachery to the state'. Their aim is to provoke 'a mass upswell against the repressive regime and all its forces' in order to preserve the 'dignity and strength of Syria' and release its spirit and awaken its 'liberal make-up'. The Islamic movement will lead the struggle against the regime and is prepared for any sacrifices. Its message to its followers is:

When trials and tribulations abound and vision is clouded and with a general futility appearing to prevail, we have to look beyond individual concerns and turn to our faith, to what the Quran has to say, to look perceptively at what history has to teach us. We must look beyond mere events and set them in their proper perspective, where a year or two has little meaning in the life of peoples and nations.

In the final analysis the day of the evil regime that rules in Syria will pass. Its symbols are mere individuals whom time will grant a few years – but who eventually will go. What remains is what matters. The reality is that truth, people and homeland still survive, that this nation is engaged in a holy struggle that will go on till the day of its resurgence and that it does so bearing two banners: Victory or Martyrdom.

To this end, which will surely come, we must increase our faith, deepen our commitment, and hold faster to God than to our personal possessions and individuality. Patience is everything.[11]

The Islamic opposition has become an umbrella sheltering several groups who resent government policies and the Baathi leaders try to do as much as possible to prove that they themselves are good Muslims and their their policies are acceptably Islamic. As early as 1950 the Syrian constitution had stated that 'Since the majority of the people of Syria belongs to the Muslim faith, the state declares its adherence to Islam and to its ideas'. The Baath could not put things so plainly and the 1964 constitution only laid down that the head of state should be a Muslim and that the state itself would respect all religions. Many Muslims considered this the separation of state and religion and some *ulama* accused the Baath of being ungodly and cried 'Either Islam or the Baath!' Asad had mixed feelings about the place of Islam in government and in the constitution of 1973 the clause stating that the head of state should be a Muslim was omitted. This aroused considerable opposition when the constitution was debated by the Council of the People, summoned specifically to discuss the draft document. The Council proposed that the clause should be reinstated and Asad, sensing that opinion was strongly against him, grudgingly agreed. While accepting the clause he wrote to the President of the Council, 'I would like to make it clear that while we may stipulate the religion of the President of the Republic, we reject every retrograde interpretation of Islam that implies a hateful puritanism and loathful fanaticism. On the contrary, Islam is a religion of love, progress and social justice, of equality.'

Since then Asad has been at pains to prove that he is a good Muslim. He has won a number of the *ulama* to his side and they have issued legal decisions confirming that Alawis are Muslims and not heretics. Others have deplored the activities of the Ikhwan stating, for example, that 'The Muslim clergy in Hama strongly condemn the criminal acts of the Muslim Brotherhood gang'. They supported the 1973 war as a religious struggle against the enemies of Islam and saw Asad as the leader in the struggle. It has been traditional in Islamic society that important religious figures support the government in power and this support often reaches the level of sycophancy. One preacher in a village mosque was heard in his sermon to claim that Muhammad was the most gifted person in history and Asad the second most gifted. He also praised the local president of the Baath party who was attending the prayers. Asad himself participates in public prayers and has made the pilgrimage to Mecca. If his opponents continue to reject his credentials and policies as a Muslim, the regime uses military force to crush opposition roused in the name of Islam – as the suppression of the uprising in Hama demonstrates. The regime hopes that its policies and successes will strength its position internally and make opposition fruitless or unnecessary. Otherwise, the Islamic banner may prove to be a rallying point for the discontented.

Notes

1 Proclamation of the UAR, 1958.
2 Syrian News Agency, 58, 7 August 1985.
3 A. A. al Marayati, *Middle Eastern constitutions and electoral laws* (New York: Praeger, 1968), p. 315.
4 Partially quoted in *Five tracts of Hasan al-Banna,* ed. C. Wendell (Berkeley: University of California, 1978), p. 36.
5 *The Times*, 13 March 1978.
6 The quotations are taken from two articles in *Middle East International*, June 1971, pp. 12–15, July 1971, pp. 13–16, by Bitar, 'The rise and decline of the Baath', and from Baath, *Texts, passim*.
7 Baath Party, report October 1965, quoted by N. Van Dam, *The struggle for power in Syria* (London : Croom Helm, 2nd edn, 1981), pp. 51–3.
8 K. Abu Jaber, *The Arab Ba'th Socialist Party* (New York: Syracuse University Press, 1966), pp. 175–83.

9   Quoted in *Al-maarifa*, 286, December 1985, p. 5.
10 Syrian Regional Command Document, 1966 (quoted by Van Dam, op. cit., p. 114).
11 *Al-nazeer*, no. 63, pp. 1–4

6 The Search for Economic Progress

> Any definition of the spirit and its values which
> does not include the impact of economic factors
> ... is inadequate and false.   (M. Aflaq)

Syria in common with other Third World countries has ambitious
plans for economic development. Also in common with other
countries it has had to face several setbacks. Some have been
self-inflicted, others have come about as a result of outside and
often uncontrollable factors. Ideology led Syria to adopt the type of
centrally planned economy which is not always conducive to
efficiency; the continuing conflict with Israel and in Lebanon means
that large amounts of finance have been devoted to the armed forces
and to the purchase of armaments – 55 per cent of current spending
and 30 per cent of total expenditure. The drop in oil prices meant
both that income from oil exports declined and that aid from oil-rich
friends diminished. These factors combined to disrupt planned
economic progress and Syria faces a critical period in its economy.

Syria had early been singled out as a country capable of great
development, with an ambitious middle class, good agricultural
prospects and a favourable environment. A World Bank team
reported in 1954 that one of the most noteworthy features of the
Syrian economy was its rapid growth during the period 1930–50 and
that agriculture and industry had both played important roles. This
expansion had stimulated commerce, transport and construction
and a substantial increase in national income had followed. In
comparison with other developing countries the rate of investment
represented 'a remarkable record of achievement. A characteristic
feature of Syria's rapid economic development [was] that it [had
been] almost wholly due to private enterprise. In spite of frequent
changes of government, private enterprise . . . retained a buoyant
outlook and continued to expand.'[1] There thus existed a sound
economic base on which to develop.

Population, Manpower Training and Planning

Syria is one of the more densely populated countries in the Middle East. It also has a high rate of population growth, 3.5 per cent annually which puts it among the highest rates in the world. (Egypt's rate is 2.5 per cent and Western Europe's less than 1 per cent.) The total population in 1982 was around 11 million which in terms of the land area is low but large stretches of the country are uninhabitable. The areas most densely inhabited are around Damascus and Aleppo and in a broad belt along the coast. This density decreases further inland and drops again until the areas on the river Euphrates are reached. As in many other developing countries migration to urban areas has been increasing rapidly although more than half the population remains rural. All cities have attracted new immigrants, with the greatest increase taking place in Damascus. It has been growing at an annual rate of more than 4 per cent – over 1 million in 1982 – and will have a projected population of 3 million in the year 2000. Aleppo had 900,000 inhabitants in 1982, projected – 2,200,000.

The country's economy is affected both by the size of population and by its movement. In addition to internal migration there has been considerable emigration to other parts of the Arab world and elsewhere. This brain drain has deprived Syria of large numbers of its skilled and semi-skilled manpower. The key to development is the availability of skilled personnel capable of planning, implementing and controlling economic growth. Syria does not yet have enough well-trained, technically and organizationally competent people and to remedy this manpower planning has assumed an increasingly important role in economic policy formation, most noticeably in the 1980–5 Development Plan. It admitted deficiencies in the past plans, which had been too ambitious, and confirmed that the evolution of the work force had failed to keep pace with the requirement of social and economic development. In other words Syria was not yet producing the right men for the right jobs. Full employment is the objective together with the distribution of workers among the different branches of economic activity in accordance with the country's plans for economic and social development. Planners recognize that improvement is needed in at least four areas; education and training; the instilling of the work ethic in society as one of its dominant values; changing attitudes towards consumerism in order to eliminate conspicuous consumption; and providing incentives to encourage enterprise and economic initiative in the public and private sectors. Syria has started in these directions but they entail fairly radical changes in society and in its attitudes. These policies would flourish best in a freer, less ideologically determined atmosphere with more incentives for private initiative. Strict planning and a controlled public sector together with a lack of political freedom hinder rather than encourage progress.

Although there is little sign of political liberalization, at the Seventh Regional Congress of the Baath party in January 1985 strong criticism was made of failures in manpower development and a decision taken to encourage the private sector. It was claimed that lack of progress was due to negligence and poor management and that the problem of the shortage of both qualified and semi-skilled manpower put the brake on rationalization and better production. Other problems compound the difficulties to be dealt with. The administration in industry is often overweighted, sometimes comprising 30 per cent of the work force, a result of the official policy of full employment (often meaning underemployment) and higher salaries for administrators. The low salaries and the undervaluing of manual workers encourage the growth of the administration. Some workers also leave public sector industry because service industries and commerce offer better wages; technicians (and even bureaucrats) leave the public sector because of state domination of the administration; they have all been trained at public expense and yet move towards the private sector (or emigrate). They experience a feeling of frustration in an atmosphere where politics dominate in the appointment of managers and in fixing targets. Management can be both authoritarian and resentful of criticism and promotion may occur only through patronage, party membership or Alawi loyalty.

Economic Growth

After the economic growth of the immediate post Second World War period there followed ten years of economic stagnation (1958–68). Thereafter a five-year period of further growth was caused by a number of factors – the beginning of oil production, income from transit fees from the oil pipeline from Iraq, investment projects and some economic liberalization, particularly after Asad came to power. The war of 1973 put a temporary stop to this expansion. It cost Syria about one billion dollars and caused much damage. Two oil refineries in Homs and oil tanks in Latakia and Tartus were bombed. Power stations in Damascus and Homs were also hit. The worst blow was the total destruction of the Banias oil terminal.

However, the years following the war were ones of great prosperity. Even the usually cautious World Bank reported that the average annual growth in the Gross Domestic Product for 1970–79 was 9 per cent, although there were significant variations in individual years. There were several reasons for this fortune – good harvests, large amounts of aid from Arab oil-producing countries after the 1973–4 oil price rise, dues from renewed oil transit fees, receipts in foreign exchange of the remittances from the many Syrians working abroad. Since then a number of factors has put pressure on the economy and by 1985–6 it was under quite considerable strain. The 1980–5 plan aimed for an annual growth in GDP of 7.6 per cent, but in 1983 according to official figures this had shrunk to 3 per cent, and according to outside observers to less than 1 per cent for the plan period. The new plan signalled a shift to more realistic and modest targets with efforts to cut imports and reduce public spending.

Agriculture

Syria is a very fertile country and could become agriculturally self-supporting given adequate investment and improved methods of irrigation and crop production. In the period 1930 to the 1950s agriculture featured prominently in the development of the country and the area under cultivation rose from 1.75 million hectares in 1938 to 3.6 million in 1953. Moreover, the irrigated area was almost doubled in the same period. There was a marked rise in agricultural production, particularly in cotton. But there were wide fluctuations (often depending on the climate) and investment gradually dropped. In 1955 agriculture accounted for the 37 per cent of the net domestic product and only 22 per cent in 1970–2. In 1975 Syria produced about three-quarters of its food consumption. It was estimated that by the end of the 1980s this will have fallen to less than half.

The Baath party government while realizing the importance of agriculture, has not always followed policies which have increased production nor has it allocated the necessary investment. First, developing countries have usually considered industrial development to be more prestigious offering quicker returns, whereas agriculture (equated with peasants and the underdeveloped countryside) is less glamorous. Peasants are conservative by inclination and have to be pushed into accepting new methods, although, if these are seen to be of benefit they are often enthusiastically adopted. Secondly, socialist ideology has led to land reform and some collectivization which have not always proved successful or relevant.

A land reform programme was first instituted in 1959 just after the union of Syria and Egypt, following the precedent set by the leaders of the Egyptian revolution. Syria had two major problems in land tenure; a few large landholders owning disproportionate amounts of land, and the splitting up of small areas among a large number of peasants. Large farms were to be expropriated and redistributed to small farmers and landless peasants who were to be organized into co-operatives. No landowner was allowed to own more than 380 hectares and over one million hectares were expropriated. State farms were also to be established. After the Baath takeover wider measures of nationalization were brought in which made the receipt of land by small farmers conditional on their joining the state controlled co-operatives. The reluctance of farmers to give up some of their independence and the enormous task of redistribution slowed down the process of land reform and the advent of Asad led to some reversal of policies. Some inefficient state farms were dismantled and the land given to the peasant co-operatives. The Asad government was more pragmatic and the performance of the farming sector began to improve.

Nevertheless, official controls on agriculture continue to be widespread and the peasant community has faced what has been called creeping rural bureaucratization. In 1980 there were more land reform measures which further reduced the size of maximum holdings. Such moves tend to discourage the private farmer and lead to more fragmentation and less efficiency. The state farms continued to be dismantled as the peasant co-operatives continued to expand. By 1982 the co-operatives accounted for some one-third of cultivated land, private farms two-thirds. While a lot of this was ideologically motivated it is still a long way from the total nationalization of land as practised under communist regimes.

The running of the co-operatives led to the usual problems encountered in bureaucratic organizations. They were set up to help to improve agricultural practices and the peasants' life by supplying credit, fertilizers, seeds, technical advice and equipment. They were to be an important instrument of change which would influence all parts of the country. The co-operative scheme has suffered some setbacks. The government is easily tempted into using them as instruments of control rather than change. Managers are often party officials rather than agricultural experts and employees are paid a fixed salary which gives them little incentive to impove production. Traditionally, peasants view with suspicion bureaucrats and government control and would rather work for themselves on their own plot of land.

Syrian planners have recognized errors in their agricultural policies. The 1980–5 plan put forward new strategies which showed where there had been shortcomings. There were plans to increase the use of irrigated land, the productivity of animal resources and the numbers of co-operatives to take in all villages. There was to be more training of peasants together with an increase in mechanization and in investment in order to achieve self-sufficiency in crops which would be produced efficiently and economically. In the 1986–90 plan efforts are underway further to increase investment in agriculture (particularly as the planned investment of the previous plan fell short). Attempts are being made to improve the production of sugar beet, fruit, milk and eggs, and sheep and cattle farming has been considerably expanded – and much more is planned in all these areas – although in 1986 wheat was imported from the United States, and imports of fruits, vegetables and meat represented about 20 per cent of total imports. The export of cotton rose from 473,000 bales in 1985 to 600,000 in 1986 and it plays an important role in the economy. The cotton-growing area has been increased to over 175,000 hectares and yields have also risen, to 3000 kilos per hectare, some 1000 kilos more than in the mid-1970s. This places Syria very near the top in world ranking. Another positive sign is the expansion in cotton ginning capacity. There are now 21 processing factories.

Euphrates Dam

Throughout the Middle East irrigation and land reclamation have been important factors in increasing agricultural production. Little progress can be made without improving irrigation. Several schemes have been undertaken with this end in view. The main project is the Tabqa Dam on the Euphrates river – comparable with Egypt's Aswan High Dam and likewise a monument to the revolution and Soviet aid and backed by a lake 80 kilometres long, bearing the name of the leader – Lake Asad. The Euphrates is Syria's major source of water and is shared with Turkey and Iraq. Irrigation in Syria was largely by direct pumping from the river and studies were made after the Second World War for projects of dam building. In the 1960s the Soviet Union offered financial and technical assistance to build a dam together with a hydroelectric station and an irrigation project. Construction began in 1968, the dam was closed in 1973 and completed in 1978. It is planned to irrigate 640,000 hectares, but problems have arisen and by 1986 only some 60,000 were being irrigated and the power station was working at 40 per cent capacity. Another problem is caused by a Turkish dam further upstream which, the Syrians claim, is taking too much water from the river and causing the level at Tabqa to drop. The planners are still optimistic and hope that the target figures will be reached and surpassed. The World Bank is helping with finance and starts have been made on several irrigation and reclamation projects on the Euphrates and elsewhere. During 1983/4 work began on a canal on the western bank of the river to serve an irrigation network designed to bring under cultivation over 300,000 hectares. The Russians began work in January 1986 on a second hydroelectric dam on the Euphrates downstream from the existing one. Much remains to be done. It is reported that only 50 of the planned 400 villages on reclaimed land have yet been built and parts of the project will show results only after several years.

Oil

Syria is not a major producer by Middle East standards but oil has played a major role in the development of the economy and world price fluctuations affect Syria's balance of trade. Oil was first struck in 1959 and began to be exported in 1968. Output rose to an annual production of some 8 million tonnes. By the end of 1986 a new field near Dair al-Zur was producing 60,000 barrels a day (planned to rise to 100,000 in 1988) which turned Syria into a net exporter.

Syria, following precedents in many parts of the world, nationalized its oil sector in 1964 under the General Petroleum Authority. Economic necessity forced a change in this policy and in 1975 contracts were signed once again with foreign companies for exploration rights. A Syrian-American consortium has to date made the most significant finds and is exploiting the Dair al-Zur field. In addition, large quantities of natural gas have been discovered which should help to compensate for any downturn which the economy may suffer in the oil sector.

In earlier times Syria had benefited in another way from oil exports when the oil pipeline had been built from Iraq through Syria to the Lebanese coast in 1934. This was later replaced in 1952 by a line of greater capacity running from Kirkuk in northern Iraq to the Syrian terminal of Banias. Transit fees provided the Syrian economy with a substantial income, although politics played havoc with the smooth running of the operation and the line was closed when relations between Iraq and Syria worsened. Income rose to 143 million dollars in 1973 when the value of oil exports was just 291 million Syrian pounds. More recently, negotiations over fees between the two rival Baath parties broke down in 1976 and Syria lost an annual income of $136 million. A new agreement reached in 1979 was broken in 1982 because of Syrian support for Iran in the Iran–Iraq war. Syria undertook to close down the line and in return Iran agreed to supply 1 million tonnes of oil free of charge and another 5 million on generous discount terms. The agreement was renewed until 1986 when disputes arose over Syria's failure to pay its debts. A deal was made with Algeria for the supply of oil on deferred terms, until a new agreement with Iran was signed in June 1986, for a six-month period only.

Industry

Until the Second World War manufacturing in Syria was largely of handicrafts although there were some traditional factories producing silk and cotton hosiery, cigarettes, flour and cement. The high prices of manufactured goods during and after the war encouraged some merchants to invest in industry, concentrating on textiles, food processing, building materials and some consumer goods. This was undertaken by private enterprise, by active members of the richer bourgeoisie who took the initiative in founding companies which achieved no little success. The World

Bank (in 1954) was quite enthusiastic about the prospects for Syrian industry. 'Considering its size and general level of development Syria already has a considerable manufacturing industry . . . Investment has been in fields where Syria should in the long run be able to achieve efficient production capable of withstanding foreign competition.' This did not mean that all Syrian industry was so efficient that it could meet unrestricted foreign competition. The World Bank noted some of the problems which faced the country and which in many ways it is still struggling to overcome. The chief need was for a skilled labour force and efficient management which could be developed only over a long period of time. Syria had, however, made an impressive start. 'Syrian industrialists. have demonstrated notable initiative and imagination in building up and managing their enterprises . . . In some plants . . . the quality of management compared favourably with that in western countries . . . costs are carefully controlled . . . some plants are extremely well equipped.'[2] There were other areas in which the picture was much less rosy and where there were serious inefficiencies.

During this period the government encouraged industry and did not interfere greatly – not surprisingly as its members were often themselves bourgeois and merchants. Between 1958 and 1965 the government became much more active and reversed previous policy. 1958 was the year in which the union began with Egypt, the country under Nasser which had introduced large scale nationalization. The ideology of state control triumphed over the causes of efficiency and profitability. The government was committed to developing an industrial economy in which a few large investors would not get rich at the expense of the population as a whole. According to the constitution of the Baath party; 'Public utilities, extensive natural resources, large industry and the means of transport are the property of the nation. The state will manage them directly and will abolish private companies and foreign concessions.' The problem in following such policies is that the 'state' is not necessarily equipped to manage and state employees do not have the same incentives to succeed as do those in private enterprise. Consequently the rate of industrial progress began to slow down and private investors ceased to play a leading role.

The core of the nationalized industry was created in 1965 when over one hundred firms were wholly or partially nationalized. The Ministry of Industry directed most of these industries, although electricity and petroleum were under separate ministries. After

1965 the government dominated the economy and controlled most developments affecting industry including planning, investment, foreign trade and pricing. Inevitably, bureaucracy took over and very little was left to individual initiative. Overall planning allocated resources, established projects and priorities. There was a lot of common sense in deciding which developments would benefit the country and the temptation to undertake large prestige projects was on the whole avoided. Syria did not try to follow the example of Egypt in establishing largely fictitious automobile, aircraft and missile industries. The emphasis was on projects to develop resources, oil and phosphates, to process local materials, textiles, sugar, cement and to produce locally, instead of importing, fertilizers, iron and steel and some consumer goods. The problems associated with nationalized industries have afflicted Syria. Central planning causes bottlenecks in supplies, under-utilized capacity, high production costs and the lack of competition means that goods are produced inefficiently in an atmosphere of low productivity.

President Asad recognizes these problems and has in theory tried to solve them. While in no way deviating from the principles of socialism and a large public sector he has liberalized some controls and encouraged a larger private sector, including foreign investors. Both local and foreign investors remain hesitant, however, fearful of government intervention and control. In practice much investment has gone into property development rather than into industry. The bulk of investment in industry has remained in government hands and despite the problems considerable progress has been made in changing the country's industrial structure. The major industries cover six main categories, textiles, food, sugar, chemicals, engineering and cement. Food and textiles accounted for two-thirds of production until 1980, after which date new developments – oil refineries, fertilizers, paper, cement – change the proportions. Industrial projects have been spread over the country in order to create development opportunities as widely as possible and to consolidate central government control wherever new enterprises are established.

Infrastructure: Electricity, Communications

The provision of electricity is one of the chief ends of Syrian industrial development. The production of electric power has risen from a million kilowatts in 1950 to 1400 million in 1974 and in 1980 after the construction of the Euphrates Dam to 4000. The 1980–5 plan aimed to connect 500,000 new customers and to light 2000 more villages. Electrification of all 100-inhabitant villages (some 5400) is planned for 1990. By the late 1970s the elements of a national electricity system were operating although shortages of electricity still constrain the development of industry. It is planned to utilize all possible water resources for generating power in order to reduce the consumption of scarce oil resources.

Together with energy developments Syria has made great efforts to improve communications throughout the country. Electricity brings the government face to the remotest village on the television screen, as roads and railways enable the physical presence to be as easily available. In 1968 there were 850 kilometres of railways; in 1980, 2000. Several new railway lines have been built with Soviet help, including those from Damascus to Jordan, Damascus to Homs, and Tartus on the coast to Aleppo. The line from Dair al-Zur to the Iraqi frontier was due for completion in 1987, presumably depending on the state of relations between the two countries. This would complete a direct link with Baghdad, built with Soviet assistance, and would virtually accomplish plans for railway development.

In 1968 Syria had 8000 kilometres of paved roads; by 1980 there were nearly 17,000. Numerous trunk and local roads have been built to link the main cities and villages, particularly Damascus with the provinces. Road and rail communications with the two main ports, Latakia and Tartus, have been greatly improved, leading to the expansion of their facilities. The third port of Banias was completed in the late 1970s for the export of petroleum products.

Finance

Syria's development projects have in most fields required large-scale financial aid for completion. This aid has been given in grants and loans by Arab countries and members of the Soviet bloc together with lesser assistance from the West. The Soviet Union and Eastern Europe have given help with irrigation, agriculture and transport schemes and with the electrification projects. France, Italy and America have helped with the development of heavy industries and oil production. Japan has contributed to two

power-generating projects. Syria's total external debt as a result of
loans reached some $3,500 million in 1986. In addition there has
been a balance of payment crisis, caused by a fall in the GDP each
year from 1984 to 1986, a standstill in the growth of remittances, a
decline in agriculture production and reduced aid following lower
oil prices. The trade deficit for 1985 was put at $900 million, and
estimated at about the same figure for 1986. Syria has had to cut
back on industrial development and there was a partial suspension
of the import of industrial equipment and raw materials for all
sectors. By 1986 several factories were running at only half their
capacity or were at a standstill. Even though aid from Arab
countries was still substantial – in 1981 it had risen as high as $1800
million – the fall in 1985/6 to less than $1000 million represented a
considerable hardship. (The country still received unpublished
amounts of aid from Saudi Arabia and elsewhere to help meet the
costs of its confrontation with Israel and its peacekeeping role in
Lebanon.) The United States cut off aid in 1983 when relations
between the two countries deteriorated during the American
intervention in Lebanon.

Remittances from Syrians working abroad have contributed
towards Syria's finances when it was estimated in the early 1980s
that there were some 400,000 emigrés, mainly in the rich Arab
states. It is not known exactly how much money has entered the
Syrian economy from these transfers (much comes in 'unofficially')
but any drop caused by workers having to return home is bound to
affect adversely the balance of payments.

The Eighth Regional Congress of the Baath Party

The congress met in January 1985 and one of the most important
items on the agenda was the economy. The Central Committee of
the party had produced a report which stressed the need to
'strengthen the economic infrastructure, promote productivity and
modernize agriculture'. The delegates to the congress did not
recommend a fundamental change in the direction of Syrian
development but they discussed the role of the private sector in the
economy and asked whether it should be increased or not. All
options backing greater public control provoked strong opposition
and the majority preferred to allow the private sector more
opportunity to compensate for the shortcomings of the public. The

final communiqué included sharp criticism of the public sector's poor performance and a call for stronger incentives for private investment. It promised a series of reforms which were designed to strengthen the operation of 'market forces'. A man who was a strong supporter of economic liberalization was appointed Minister of Economy and Foreign Trade and a campaign was opened to attract more foreign investment.

The future for the Syrian economy remains unsure and affected by a number of imponderable factors and the planners have had to scale down targets, reduce expenditure and curb imports. It has yet to be seen what effect if any the more liberal policy towards the private sector will have. The Baath party is committed to raising economic standards for all its citizens but the constraints of external factors and of its own policies make the economic future uncertain.

Notes

1 International Bank for Reconstruction and Development, *The economic development of Syria* (Baltimore: Johns Hopkins University, 1955) pp. 18–23.
2 ibid., pp. 104–6.

7 The Pursuit of Education

Education is the greatest weapon in the hand of the
revolution.   (M. Aflaq)

Education in a Developing Society

Education is the foundation of all development, in society, the
economy and culture. Nothing of value can be achieved in the
absence of an educated public, and the more highly educated the
better. Education is the way in which societies pass knowledge on to
new generations, preserve already existing values and introduce
change. Institutions of education regulate the flow of scientific
information into society and control the quality and kind of
knowledge it acquires. Through their activities, these institutions
add to the national cultural wealth and improve a country's
capabilities to use efficiently its natural, human and financial
resources. Educational activities work in this positive sense and at
the same time they disturb traditional values and weaken outdated
institutions. Education is one of the major factors contributing to
change that has already taken place and is the key to nation building
and the basis for future economic development and social change.
The importance of education is recognized by political leaders who
are determined to keep the educational system under their control,
to set national standards and to monitor the ideas transmitted by
teachers. It is a major method of gaining legitimacy among the
young and of instilling concepts of authority and obedience.

The faith in modern education is derived from several factors –
notably that universities and schools have been the channels for
transmitting those ideas and values which have so influenced
traditional society, that reformers and modernizers have often been
the products of these institutions, and that developing countries are
in urgent need of the skilled and highly trained personnel which
only such institutions can produce.

The traditional aim of an education has been to produce the complete man, a cultured person in the broadest sense of that term, open to all ideas and capable of appreciating different aspects of culture and of contributing himself to its development. The authoritarian, ideologically motivated society tries to produce highly educated men who do not question and criticize the ideas and principles of the ruling group. The ideal educated man is he who unquestioningly accepts government policy and is willing to co-operate in putting it into operation, and who acts only according to the conclusions and directives of others.

There are stages through which countries pass in the attempt to achieve educational efficiency. Traditional societies use education as the means of preserving traditional values and the customary way of life. There is no interest in or conception of change. Such a system is authoritarian where the teacher's authority is unquestioned and the emphasis is laid on the reproduction of memorized facts. This method stunts initiative and the attitudes instilled at school are carried over into working life, the desire not to disturb the system and a reluctance to assume authority. Educational systems pass from this stage into one where there is more criticism of the received wisdom and accepted practices. Students move from memorizing to trying to understand what they learn. Facts are no longer accepted as immutable truths. The aims of education change; it becomes a means of social betterment, for improving the quality of life and for understanding better the functioning of society. The final stage in this development is the growth of the ability to initiate changes according to the particular needs of society. The goal becomes that of trying to meet the needs of the country in its specific circumstances. Graduates are looked upon as creative thinkers and future leaders.

Universities as centres of research and innovation seek new knowledge which modifies, improves or replaces the old. Curricula change in order to meet the demands of changing needs. An innovative educational system influences society in adopting and accepting positive change. It is in hoping to achieve this latter stage that authoritarian states are trapped. They need to produce creative graduates who accept unquestioningly ideas and policies. The concepts of authoritarianism and creative development are often at odds and the state has either to accept the obedient, unimaginative, uncritical employee lacking initiative and creativity, or tolerate the creative and productive technologist, civil servant or artist who may at the same time criticize government policy.

Baath Ideology towards Development and Education

In the words of Michel Aflaq: 'Students combine two essential and revolutionary qualities: youth and education. Revolution is by nature a youthful spirit, the spirit of revolution is the spirit of rebellion. It is the spirit of the soul, the warm hope which moves man to aspire to perfection and all this is expressed by youth. Education is the greatest weapon in the hand of the revolution for its transforms the revolution and transforms the revolutionary hopes and objectives from sentiments and vague wishes into a high degree of clear consciousness, and planned and organized consciousness.'[1] It is unclear quite what Aflaq is saying here about education. The Baath Party Constitution adopted in 1947 put the matter more firmly:

> The educational policy of the party aims at the creation of a new Arab generation which believes in the unity of the nation, in the eternity of its mission. This policy, based on scientific reasoning, will be freed from the shackles of superstitions and reactionary traditions; it will be imbued with the spirit of optimism, of struggle, and of solidarity among all citizens in the carrying out of a total Arab revolution, and in the cause of human progress. Therefore the party decides as follows: Teaching is one of the exclusive functions of the state. Therefore, all foreign and private educational institutions are abolished. Education at all stages shall be free for all citizens. Primary and secondary education shall be compulsory. Professional schools with the most modern equipment shall be established, where education shall be free. Teaching careers and all that relates to education are set aside for Arab citizens. An exception to this rule is made in the instance of higher education.

These articles and the preamble add more precision to the ideology of education and set the path which Baath governments have tried to follow. There is little to stamp them as particularly Baathist apart from the obvious insistence on their Arab character. The Constitution of 1964 added: 'Education is a right of every citizen. The state is interested in the growth of a generation strong in body, mind and character, with faith in its spiritual heritage and pride in its Arab virtues.'

The Constitution of 1973 restated the principles of education:

> The national socialist culture shall be the basis of building up the unified socialist Arab society. It shall aim at enhancing moral values, realizing the ideals of the Arab nation, developing society, serving human causes, and encouraging artistic talents and physical education. Science, scientific research and all scientific achievements constitute a main prop for the progress of Arab socialist society. The state shall give it full support. Education shall be a right guaranteed by the state. It shall be free in all stages and compulsory in the primary steps. The state shall endeavour to make other stages compulsory, and shall supervise education and direct it in a manner which ensures its adaptation to the needs of society and production. The educational and cultural system shall aim to bring up a national Arab generation who are socialist and scientific in their manner of thinking, attached to their land and history, proud of their heritage, and imbued with the spirit of struggling to realize the aims of the nation of unity, liberty, and socialism and of contributing to the service and progress of humanity. The educational system shall ensure the continued progress of the people and shall meet the needs of their continued social, economic, and cultural development.

Educational Planning

Education has formed an important element in Syria's five-year plans, where the path that society is expected to follow is carefully defined. 1980 was taken as the basic year for establishing a long-range development strategy in ten- and five-year frames up to the year 2000. The underlying philosophy of comprehensive planning aims at the achievement of Arab unity politically and economically, and the consolidation of socialism. The planners wish to achieve stable self-development based on the right kind of social behaviour and on the construction of the socialist system. This requires a stable economic and social strategy that will utilize all available human, financial and natural resources. All these developments require a skilled, educated and committed population and therefore education is given priority.

To overcome past failures society in 2000 will require the application of the concept of comprehensive planning, giving priority to the building of the material socialist basis of the country, eradicating illiteracy and functional illiteracy amongst workers by spreading culture for the masses which would help to raise both their cultural awareness and their productive potential. Every citizen should be made aware that his personal interests are linked closely to those of his society. Through education consecutive generations will come to value order and discipline, to love work and its performance at the required level of ability. Thus the power of individuals and the masses to carry out research and invention will increase. Social action will be a scientific, political and popular impulse uncovering hidden potentials, overcoming obstacles and causing purposeful changes in the social structure of the country.

While such concepts may cause a shudder, there is no doubt about the kind of society Syrian planners wish to see in the year 2000. It is nothing less than the transformation of present society and the creation of the new Arab socialist man committed to the principles of Baathism. And because of the heterogeneous nature of the Syrian population one of the basic aims of education is to produce the Syrian man with loyalties to state and party and to Arabdom rather than to region, group or sect. A national educational system fairly distributed is the way to achieve this aim. The peasant's son in the village must have the same educational opportunities as the lawyer's son in Damascus. Schools, colleges and universities are being spread throughout the country to try to reduce regional loyalty and disparities and to reduce the rural-urban migration which depopulates the countryside and contributes to urban overcrowding. Population movements disturb planning predictions and are difficult to control, as is the rapid growth of population which upsets planned expansion in schools and universities.

Government and Education

In a centrally planned state education is centrally directed. In Syria it is primarily the responsibility of the Ministries of Education and of Higher Education, with a limited role now exercised by the private sector and UNRWA which runs primary and intermediate schools for the Palestinians. The Ministry of Education controls all pre-university education (only secondary agricultural schools come under the Ministry of Agriculture) in addition to the two-year post-secondary institutes, which train teachers for various subjects, and institutes which train technicians at the assistant engineer level. Curricula and major policies are set at ministry level although there is some limited participation in policy making and administration at the local level through the directorates of education in each region (*muhafaza*). Implementation of these programmes which are the same throughout the country is in the hands of the inspectorates. Private schools are strictly controlled by the ministry which appoints the head in each school.

The Ministry of Higher Education is responsible for most institutes of higher education. Liaison is maintained with these institutes through the Council of Higher Education under the minister and consists of university rectors, deputy ministers, representatives of teachers and students. The council has responsibilities for planning, policy, funding, admissions and co-ordination.

The Historical Background

Until the middle of the nineteenth century education was largely in the hands of religious teachers, either in traditional Quranic schools or in the few classes run by priests or nuns, often little more than a small group of boys around one uneducated teacher. Education was gradually extended as Ottoman state schools were introduced in mid-century and as local Christian communities and foreign missionaries increased their activities. Although Ottoman expenditure on education was very small, Syria acquired more state schools than did other Arab provinces. Nevertheless, most Syrians remained illiterate. The two universities in the area were in Beirut, but in Damascus a school of medicine was inaugurated in 1903 and a school of law some ten years later. Both were closed during the First World War. Under the Arab government of Faisal 1918–20, despite its short duration, several steps were taken to try to improve the education system. Schools were Arabized, the training of teachers undertaken and a plan for the development of education was studied. Thirty-six new schools were opened in Damascus and

Aleppo and an agricultural school was established. The law school and medical college were reopened as the nucleus of Damascus University.

These promising developments received a severe setback when the French began their Mandate. They dismantled the education expansion programme begun by the Arab government, closed down local schools and allowed them to reopen only if they adopted a French-approved curriculum which made the study of the French language compulsory. They devoted a very small proportion of the budget to education. During the Mandate an average of seventeen new primary schools was established each year and the number of pupils about tripled. By 1944, the last year of French control of the school system, less than a quarter of school-age children (6–12) attended school. There were only thirteen public secondary schools with fewer than 5,000 pupils. Some 80 per cent of the population remained illiterate. Private schools gave education a sectarian, foreign rather than a national basis. Education remained a privilege rather than a right and the small educated élite developed very slowly.

The Mandate government had decided in 1920 to keep open the school of law and was eventually persuaded to maintain the medical school. In 1923 an institution combining the two schools was established as the Syrian University. Only one other department was added in 1929 (the short-lived higher school of letters) as the French hindered the expansion of a national university. The number of students in medicine and law grew from 180 in 1919 to 1094 in 1944. The year 1922 saw the first enrolment of girls of whom there were in 1945 72 in medicine and 12 in law.

Immediately after independence there was a great expansion in education. Syrian governments of all tendencies have made strenuous efforts to foster education. Between 1970 the proportion of the state budget devoted to education ranged between 13 and 20 per cent and by 1967 the proportion of the population receiving education was 17 per cent. Vocational education developed on a smaller scale. University education grew rapidly after 1955 and the numbers of students in institutes of higher education per 100,000 inhabitants was 86 in 1950 and 590 in 1966. By 1966 education had apparently made great strides yet was beset by a number of problems. The chief of these was the attempt to transform Syria into a modern developed state when, according to the official census, of employed persons over 60 per cent were illiterate, 22 per cent had a secondary diploma and 1 per cent a university degree. Moreover, those with an education did not always have relevant knowledge. Syrian educators had given the educational system an Arab and Syrian orientation while retaining the French concept that the aim of education was to prepare an élite, with an emphasis on general culture and theoretical knowledge. Graduates were prepared chiefly for government offices.

Private schools continued to play a role, those established by religious sects, nationality groups or foreign missions, particularly in intermediate and secondary education. They took 31 per cent of students at these levels in 1966. By imparting a sectarian or particularist view to the students they helped to perpetuate factionalism and no long-term policy of assimilating these schools into the public system was adopted. They remained important as long as the public schools could not accommodate all students.

The ambitious aim at the time was to abolish illiteracy within 10 years; this proved to be entirely unfeasible. Even universal primary education does not necessarily eradicate illiteracy as children, particularly among peasants, are kept away from school for domestic and field work and children who leave school early quickly relapse into semi-literacy. Nor was education directed to meeting the large and growing need for technically qualified graduates. In intermediate schools mathematics and science subjects took only 23 per cent of the curriculum and technical subjects a mere 6 per cent. Technical education was separate from general education and was regarded as second best. Only those who could not continue general education entered technical schools. The number of technical students was some 8–12 per cent of the total secondary body.

Higher education showed a similar bias and was not geared to the needs of the country. The majority of students read arts and humanities, and Islamic law, although employment opportunities in these fields were scarce. Posts in technical fields remained unfilled. A striking example of unbalance was provided in agriculture were 60 per cent of the population gained their livelihood and where 2–3 per cent of university students specialized in it. Only 3–4 per cent studied medicine and slightly more science and engineering.

Education in the First Years of the Baath 1966–1970

Building an educational system is a long-term project and under the early Baath leadership progress was slow in politicizing education, although many moves were ideologically motivated. An important early reform was state control of the private schools. A decree of 1967 left ownership of these schools in private hands and placed their management in the hands of the Ministry of Education and required the use of official textbooks and curricula at all levels. Early resistance to these measures soon subsided. Other reforms tried to eliminate any kind of élitism by opening secondary schools to all, even though there were not enough schools, particularly in rural areas. Curricula were altered to include more mathematics, science and practical subjects and by 1969 10 per cent of secondary graduates had studied science. Technical education received a higher priority and the attempt was made to introduce a new ethos into this area – with the motto 'knowledge for the sake of work' – and respect for work and production was encouraged. Intermediate institutes for different specialities were developed to train the needed personnel in the intermediate ranks. Agriculture received more attention and the number of secondary agricultural schools increased to ten. A one-year course for graduates of these schools was introduced at the Institute for Developing the Countryside. In addition, facilities for higher technical and scientific training were expanded with five Higher Technical Institutes. New universities were opened in Aleppo, offering scientific and other facilities, and in Latakia specializing in sciences. Larger numbers of students studied abroad, mostly in the West during this earlier period, and this also led to an increase in the brain drain. The annual rate of loss of skilled manpower increased fivefold between 1956 and 1967. Some 10 per cent of students who studied abroad did not return. Plans to induce them to return did not really materialize.

At primary school level progress was not as fast as had been hoped. In 1960 the first Five-Year Plan aimed to raise the proportion of 6–12-year-olds at school from 43 to 77 per cent but by 1971 this figure had reached only 60–80 per cent of boys and 47 per cent of girls. The Third Plan wanted to increase the overall percentage to 80. The shortage of qualified teachers, overcrowded classes and lack of adequate schools slowed progress.

The failure to reduce illiteracy hampered social and economic progress. In 1960 60 per cent of the population (over ten-years-old) was illiterate. In the following eight years this proportion declined to only 59 – 41 per cent among males, 77 per cent among females. A mass literacy campaign was tried through various popular organizations, labour and peasant unions, youth and women's federations. To succeed it would have needed a huge popular effort mobilized behind a total acceptance of the government and its policies. Industrial workers were the prime target and workers had to prove their literacy to be eligible for trade union committees and offices. It was far more difficult to educate peasants and women at home although efforts were made through television and radio. The pessimistic forecast in 1970 was that at the prevailing rate of progress it would take 150 years to eliminate illiteracy!

The Educational System

Primary Level

Primary education is compulsory and free. It lasts for six years from age 6. Although legally compulsory no strict measures have been taken to implement the law. Nevertheless there has been considerable success in increasing numbers of students – in 1960 482,000 and in 1980 1,500,000, an increase of some 400 per cent. Girls come out disadvantaged in these figures; 77 per cent of female children are enrolled and 96 per cent male. In rural areas these figures are somewhat lower (72 per cent female). The factors which hinder full enrolment are the high rate of population growth, nomadicism, lack of facilities in remote areas and certain social attitudes towards the education of girls in some rural areas or families.

Intermediate (Preparatory) Level

All pupils who have successfully completed the primary level are eligible to enter the intermediate schools. This level lasts for three years (ages 12–14) and is free but not compulsory. Additional subjects of study include foreign languages, science and political studies. Since 1970 the five-year plans have included the objective of merging the primary and intermediate levels into a single level of basic education yet this aim was unfulfilled in the Fifth Plan. Numbers of students rose from 65,000 in 1960 to 418,000 in 1980, an increase of 540 per cent. The ratio of male to female was 268,000 to 150,000. Despite this very large rise the net enrolment was still low, some 66 per cent. It is also the unfulfilled aim of the plan to make intermediate education compulsory.

Secondary Level

This level lasts three years, ages 15–17. Entry is selective based on the results of examination. There are two streams: the general and the technical. The general stream is by far the more popular taking 86 per cent of students at secondary level in 1980. Students who are 15 years old are free to choose either general or technical, but those beyond this age must enter technical schools.

Vocational-Technical Training

There are some sixty institutions in various technical and vocational fields, known as intermediate institutes. They offer a two-year course (sometimes longer) for students who have gained the Baccalaureat. In 1980 there was a total enrolment of 23,000. They offer training for technicians who are essential for the socio-economic development of the country. The best graduates of the technical secondary schools are admitted to engineering programmes. There is a continuing need to increase the proportion of students entering technical training, often regarded as an inferior form of education in which those enrol who are unsuccessful in general education. Other obstacles have been the lack of well-trained instructors, of female students and of well-defined policy towards technical education.

Traditionally the reluctance in Syria to follow technical and vocational training arose as it usually led to manual employment. Syrians like people elsewhere prefer white-collar occupations. Studies amongst Arab youth on their attitudes towards work and vocational education and the impact of socio-economic factors on their attitudes reveal that the vast majority do not want to do manual labour. Even more significant is the fact that students surveyed in vocational training preferred occupations unrelated to their training. These social and educational factors have slowed down the expansion of technical education together with the high costs involved in establishing technical institutes. Vocational training has tended to attract the drop-outs of the general educational system and the academically less intelligent, and has carried the stigma of being the last resort of those unsuccessful in educational terms.

Nevertheless, the shift from general academic to vocational and technical education is fundamental to the process of development. It is impossible for Syria to develop without taking into account the human resources that are available and there are signs in the latest Syrian plan that this is happening. In early education the aim is 'modify tuition in order to include classes for the gradual introduction of manual labour and set up programmes inspired by the needs and conditions of the environment'. There is the shift to different types of technical training more suited to Syrian needs together with the running down of other subjects. The aim is to have 60 per cent of students from the preparatory stage join the work force after technical and professional training. In addition foreign scholarships are offered in technical subjects unavailable in Syrian institutes. Numerous new technical institutions were to be opened according to the 1980–5 Plan: 45 secondary technical and 5 secondary commercial schools. In existing institutions there will have to be a change of emphasis. There will be a particular move from general education to a technical scientific one. The aim was to increase the output of students from technical and vocational schools from the 1975 level of 3,200 to about 7,500 in 1985.

Higher Education

There are four universities with a total enrolment in 1980 of 95,000 (70,000 males, 25,000 females). Damascus University, the largest and oldest, has 14 faculties, Aleppo 7, Tishrin in Latakia 5, and al-Baath University in Homs (founded 1979) 5. In addition, there is the recently founded Baath Party Higher Institute for Political Science, a university-level institute. Damascus covers a wide range of subjects in the arts and sciences, the latter including medicine with 14 departments and various hospitals. The faculty of Islamic Law is the facility in Syria at the higher education level for the preparation of religious teachers. Other faculties include agriculture, commerce, engineering, science and dentistry. The other universities provide more limited facilities, although Aleppo oversees other institutes – for agriculture, medicine and engineering. Latakia operates an agricultural institute and plans to provide programmes mainly in science and technology. Several university technical institutes are planned in mechanical and electrical engineering, computer science, energy and commerce.

A university education is not the only means of advancement in life. It is, however, often seen as such by society and the Syrian government has been unwilling to disappoint students by restricting the numbers of entrants to university. This has led to untenable situations in which hundreds of students attempt to attend lectures, where little real teaching or education can take place, where semi-educated graduates are produced and hundreds of graduates are offered non-productive government posts. The policy of open admissions is possible when students graduating from secondary schools are in manageable numbers. Democratization of education and the open door policy with free tuition have led to mass higher education. The great pressure on universities has exceeded most of the expected projections.

The drawbacks at university level are those experienced at other levels – the over-large classes, inadequate facilities, over-emphasis on the reproduction of knowledge and examination passing. Students complain that on graduation they are not good engineers or computer programmers, but that they have learned how to pass examinations. There is strict political control. The Baath party controls university admission and the only political activities allowed are those sponsored by the party. Indoctrination begins early in life (in the vanguards of the Baath party) and one of the ways to advance in the hierarchy is to inform on teachers and fellow students at home and abroad. Official forms are handed out for completion and the following is an example:

Arab teachers and revolutionary educationalists!
We are living through a critical period of our glorious history. Colonialist influences are trying to divide the nation and keep it in a slough of backwardness and ignorance. Since you are the mirror that reflects the progress made in our great country, and bear considerable responsibility in this regard, we look to you, through your alertness and awareness in the country where you are, to be a loyal servant of your own nation and the Syrian Revolution and to keep us informed of the following:
(1) The political situation – parties – associations – fronts and their associated activities.
(2) The economic situation.
(3) The social situation.
(4) Guerrilla organizations and their roles.
(5) Foreign activity against the Arab cause and Arab interests.
(6) Zionist activity in the country in which you are working.

Its forms, techniques, and any persons you know who are working in this field.

(7) Those working against Syria and the Arab cause in all fields.

(8) Rumours circulating about Syria.

(9) The names of male and female teachers known to you, of all nationalities; their political tendencies and conduct.

(10) An appreciation of how the authorities look at Syria and the Arab cause, and their academic and information practices.

(11) Any confirmed incident known to you or witnessed by you that concerns Syria.

(12) Difficulties that you have had to face during your year of academic secondment.

Such control inhibits a free academic atmosphere and hinders research. Perhaps the most sensitive area is that of sending students abroad for study. They may acquire unsound ideas or opt to remain away and politically 'sound' countries cannot always offer the kind of training sought. Nevertheless, the plan provided for 3268 scholarships abroad in engineering, human and basic sciences and (unspecified) basic studies at undergraduate and graduate level.

An interesting sidelight on the factor of political control is that in 1985 Algeria withdrew its seconded students from Syrian universities, alleging that the Baath party was attempting to exert political influence over them and to interfere in their lives and social affairs. The same irony is apparent in university life as in industry and government in that political stability and control are achieved at the expense of efficiency, initiative and forward thinking.

Brain Drain

The so-called brain drain is a tangible expression of discontent, whether with the political system or the opportunities, prestige and job satisfaction offered by Syrian society. Those emigrating are highly trained and qualified personnel, often but not always trained abroad. They are usually of great value to their own country – doctors, engineers, teachers. In a sense the drain is proof of the efficacy of the educational system in that these graduates are welcome elsewhere. A proportion of the migrational flow from

Syria is to other Arab countries, usually the OPEC countries of Arabia and the Gulf. The slowing down of oil revenues will mean that these countries will have to lessen their dependence on foreign personnel and that some Syrians will have to return home to be reintegrated or move elsewhere. Others emigrate to Europe and the United States and usually settle. In 1976 for example, the United States admitted 130 professional and technical Syrian workers, largely doctors and engineers.

The Syrian government has attempted to stem this flow by insisting that graduates who have been financed publicly spend some years in Syria after graduation in nominated occupations. However, graduates do not produce good work if forced to stay against their will in posts or areas they find uncongenial. They may be frustrated by political control, lack of facilities or inefficiency. They may also wish to avoid military service. The government is in a dilemma, needing their services and yet not wishing to encourage possible centres of opposition. Some find suitable employment in the private sector.

Women's Education and Employment

Syria is attempting to integrate women fully into the educational and economic systems. The government is committed to equality of opportunity although the numbers of males in education still far exceed those of females. Traditional attitudes hinder full integration – male dominance, family conservatism, religious opposition. The government has granted women by law equal job opportunities, rights and privileges, yet women are not often attracted into vocational and technical schools. The plan does make provision for women entrants into certain branches of engineering, into medicine, and into the more traditionally female areas such as nursing or domestic science. The government is not inhibited, as is the Saudi, by official discriminatory policies, and in order to achieve the planned development it cannot neglect the female half of the population. The literacy rate of 25 per cent of all women is higher than that of Egypt, Iraq, or Jordan.

The Armed Forces and Education

It is difficult to obtain information on the forces' needs and the relevance of the educational system to those needs. There are three sources of military training, the university and specialized technical institutes, military academies, and training abroad, at present entirely in Eastern bloc countries. It is likely that some of the new courses and facilities introduced in the plan, computer facilities, electronic engineering, are thought relevant to military use and engineers and other highly skilled technicians have to serve two years in the army and another three years working where the government sends them.

The Syrian army has increased dramatically in size (1947, 10,000 men; 1984, 362,000) and the amount in the budget allotted to it has risen equally. The proportion of the working population in the army rose from 2.3 per cent in 1965 to 6.3 per cent in 1975. Observers have noted the marked improvement in the technical and tactical qualities of the Syrian soldier, which is obviously a result of better education and training, and of the sophisticated weapons that can be operated reliably even by non-technically skilled soldiers. The regime relies on the loyalty of the army which is heavily involved in politics and expenditure on it has been at the expense of welfare-related spending, health and education.

Reforms, Policies and their Effect

The long-term aim of Baath educational policy is to transform society, not only ideologically but also economically and technologically. As has been stated, the regime gives top priority to creating a strong army, to achieve parity with Israel and to ensure political stability at home and counter possible opposition. The army can ensure immediate compliance; educating the population into loyalty and into having a vested interest in the *status quo* is a much longer-term process. Students and parents see education as *the* means of advancement in society and choose those studies which are thought best to guarantee this. This entails a possible conflict with government aims in a society where a graduate government civil servant (even if underemployed) carried more prestige than a skilled non-graduate technician.

Some educationally induced changes in society are opposed by the traditional sectors. Islamic resentment over the secular policies of the Baath has already been serious. Criticism published clandestinely is severe, accusing the Baath of wishing to destroy the traditional 'structure of Syrian society thus ensuring a longer period of control', by educating children negatively 'so as to destroy their intellects, undermine civilized behaviour and kill off any aspirations in the cradle'. 'Evidently in the long term this policy will deprive Syrian society of much-needed skills and academic and scientific knowledge and keep it in the backwaters of civilized development.' There is also strong resentment against the policies towards women which are considered anti-Islamic. For example, the order for girls to remove their head coverings in young women's camps is bitterly criticized. The Baath line was: 'If a girl insists on retaining it [head covering] this shows up her reactionism . . . [which is not] in line with our mission of Unity, Freedom and Socialism.'

While Muslim opposition has been open and sometimes violent, middle-class opposition has been more muted, although the government has admitted the value of the middle classes by allowing more private enterprise. They do not all favour the public school system and were often those who in the past sent their children to private schools. Those who have the means or the connections can send their children abroad to study. (US figures estimate that each year 7000 Syrians study in American universities, probably most sent privately. There were 3000–5000 in Russia, and 3000–4000 in Eastern European states, at government expense.) That not all government social and educational policies are succeeding is underlined by the fact that in the 1980–5 Plan studies were to be made of, and the authorities helped to fight, the causes of juvenile delinquency and youth vagrancy.

The Syrian government is making serious efforts to improve the educational system to make it fit the needs of the twenty-first century. Care has been taken to make education relevant to planned development. These are long-term projects and reforms are slow to take effect. True education breeds the questioning mind. It remains to be seen how far the Baathi regime will welcome the advent of constructive criticism.

Note

1   Baath, *Texts*, pp. 154–5.

8   The Growth of Culture

> We have to restore to words their meaning, their
> strength and their sacredness.   (M. Aflaq)

Culture is at the root of a country's character and life. Baathi
thinkers have characterized the Arab nation above all as

> . . . a cultural reality. Culture is the whole Arab cultural heritage;
> it is a communal view of the feeling for the future. The Arabs are
> bound together by language and history, and culture has validity
> for them only if it is an expression of Arabness and expressed in
> Arabic. The development of Arab culture is the mission and duty
> of every Arab. It has to be freed from the shackles imposed on it
> by its past colonial history. Every Arab will share in the cultural
> awakening.
>   We are in need of the formation of the free, responsible,
> independent, self-conscious Arab individual. We need the crea-
> tion of the Arab man, for the humane view in our milieu has been
> almost non-existent.[1]

This idea was enshrined in the original Baath party constitution of
1947:

> The Party seeks to develop a general national culture for the
> whole Arab fatherland which shall be Arab, liberal, progressive,
> extensive, profound and humanist . . . The state is responsible
> for the protection of liberty of speech, of publication, of
> assembly, of protest and of the press . . . Intellectual work is one
> of the most sacred kinds. It is the state's concern to protect and
> encourage intellectuals and scientists. Within the limits of the
> Arab national idea, every freedom will be given for the founda-
> tion of clubs . . . as well as for obtaining profit from the cinema,
> radio, television and all the other facilities of modern civilization
> in order to spread generally the national culture.

This seems to promise complete freedom for the artist to express his ideas, even if they are those of protest. The state is given a prominent role in this process and perhaps the restricting phrase 'within the limits of the Arab national idea' gives scope for the suppression of critical ideas. Certainly the principles expressed in the constitution of 1973 begin to narrow down the field of activity of the artist: 'The national socialist culture shall be the basis of building up the unified socialist Arab society. It shall aim at . . . encouraging artistic talents.' Finally, in the 1980–5 Plan society is urged to give priority to building the material socialist basis of the country and 'every citizen should be made aware that his personal interests are linked closely to those of his society'. Despite the guarantee of freedom of thought, these latter sentiments come close to stating that all art must contribute to the development of the state's vision of society. Many artists in the developing world would agree that art should be *committed*, that it should make a positive contribution to the welfare of their country and that they, as intellectuals, have a responsibility to foster an understanding of its problems and to encourage education in its broadest sense.

A Syrian writer and sociologist has expressed his feelings on commitment very clearly:

> Contemporary Arab writers have been preoccupied with themes of struggle, revolution, liberation, emancipation, rebellion, alienation. A writer could not be a part of Arab society and not concern himself with change. To be oblivious to tyranny, injustice, poverty, deprivation, victimization, repression, is insensitively proper. I would even say that writing about Arab society without concerning oneself with change is a sort of *engagement* in irrelevances.[2]

The writer admits that his aims for society as a novelist are revolutionary.

This commitment does not mean that the artist necessarily accepts the ideology of party or state but that he agrees in general that his art should be positive in the sense of contributing to the process of the formulation of ideas and policies. It should criticize, argue, suggest and is rarely satisfied with the status quo. There has been much dispute over the role of the artist in society and while there are always party hacks, others feel helpless to contribute to change. A leading Syrian writer believes that 'We deceive ourselves

if we believe that a literary work written and published in a country
70 per cent illiterate can change political and social life. It is up to
the political organization . . . not the literary novel . . . to change
the existing situation.'[3] The state has in its turn made efforts to
encourage art and promote literature, yet the artist by his very
nature and calling stands apart from society, feeling alienated and
unable to do very much other than experiment in his particular
genre. He works in the realm of his ideas which he launches into
society, not knowing whether they will be accepted or have any
effect. In the end, however, art stands or falls on its intrinsic merit,
and not on whether it purveys certain political ideas.

As part of its effort to promote culture the state encouraged the
formation of the Union of Arab Writers which publishes its own
journal, organizes conferences and maintains contacts with writers
in other Arab countries. The Ministry of Culture with a system of
cultural centres attempts to spread culture throughout the country.
The 1980–5 Plan proposed to provide such centres in all parts of the
country varying from 'rooms in the village to a palace in the capital'.
In these centres lectures are given on aspects of culture, and
performances and exhibitions are held. A glance at the contents
pages of two of the official literary and cultural publications shows
the wide range of topics treated: technology in Syria; the real, the
imaginary, the ideological in the modern Arabic novel; towards an
Arab strategy for the book; innovative writing.

That the state takes culture very seriously is shown in an article on
'the cultural presence' in one of the literary journals by the Minister
of Culture herself.

> The Arab fatherland, despite all the difficulties through which it
> is passing, has been able to maintain a cultural presence in the
> world, to widen and develop it, to carve the name of Arabdom on
> the tablet of human existence, through the struggle of our nation
> and its steadfastness, through its ability to penetrate the blockade
> which enemies impose – both the imperialists and Zionists. I do
> not claim that culture alone can undertake this penetration.
> Rather culture is a basic element in politics and it plays a principal
> role in the struggle for national liberation and social progress, for
> the change which is one of the great aims of culture . . . For this
> reason culture has a part in the great role of Syria, as an important
> agent in its policy, its struggle, its science and work . . . And
> today, on the admission of Arab colleagues and foreign visitors

and the masses of our people, it is a culture which is far-reaching
in its leadership and influence, which aims to work in the service
of the people and to spread from one end of the Arab region to
the other.[4]

In Baathi ideology Syrian culture is a part of the Arab whole. In
what follows the works of leading Syrian writers have been selected
for discussion. Some of them, although born in Syria, have worked
mainly outside the country, usually in Beirut which has served as the
publishing centre for the whole of the Arab world. In this sense,
some writers are representing the Arab world rather than specifically the Syrian. Until recently writers moved to Beirut to publish their
work in order to escape the censorship of their own governments. It
was a place of experimentation, of the avant-garde and to some
extent of free speech. The writers who remain at home have often to
be more guarded in what they write, placing their work in another
era or in an allegorical context. The Arab world's leading poet,
Adunis, is a case in point. Born in Syria, he has spent most of his
working life in Beirut and has published his poetry there.

Prose Writing

All forms of literature have flourished in Syria since the Second
World War – poetry, drama and prose, particularly the short story.
Four or five writers stand out in this context – one of the best known
is Zakariya Tamir. His career is typical of several Arab writers –
self-education, government employ and exile. He was born in
Damascus in 1931 and he worked for sometime as a craftsman
before he took to writing and journalism. He headed the television
drama department (1967–70), and edited a government journal –
that of the Ministry of Culture – until he left for London in 1981. He
belongs to a group of writers who began their careers in the
mid-1950s under the influence of modernist European trends and
the attempts to adapt those trends to local circumstances. In the
1960s after the trauma of the 1967 war, realism in his writing was left
behind and he moved into a world of fantasy.

In two early stories, published in Beirut in 1959, *A carnation for
the weary asphalt* and *Summer* he displays both a surrealistic
imagination and a melancholy weariness with life in the city and its
attendant noise and crowds. As an observer he seems unable to

cope, shies away from commitment and does not try to participate in or attempt to change things. In both stories relations between the sexes play an important role and are treated in a frank manner – at least for that time and that society. In *Summer* the hero Majid wants to make love to his fiancée Itaf before they are married. Below in the street a policeman waves on a speeding woman motorist who ogles him, and he is reminded of his cold wife. A grocer feels strongly attracted to a servant girl who flirts with him. The sun beats down on the deserted streets. Majid gets his way and Itaf immediately urges him to marry her. He is now repelled and blames everything on the life of the city. He ponders: 'When shall we get married? I feel distaste for this question. She has given herself to me and now she's demanding the price – marriage. Everything in my city has its set price – no one gives anything without wanting something in return. All of them are merchants of a new high class type . . . they are spread round wearing different masks. I hate this kind of person. I hate them madly and now I find out that Itaf is one of them.' He cannot cope and walks away through the tired, scorching streets.

In the *Carnation* a young girl, still a virgin, lies in bed thinking sadly and listening to the sounds of the street. The face of her mother appears and warns her: 'All men worship a woman humbly when they catch her scent, but turn away in disgust the moment their desire is fulfilled.' The scene changes to the street where men are following a coffin under the hot sun. Two friends in the cemetery discuss death. 'Death is a haven for those who grow old.' 'We too will grow old . . . we won't always be young.' 'Why are you talking like this?' 'I hate the day, the light which shows everything up, the noise, the harsh sun, the crowds . . . all of it makes me think continually of death. Perhaps soon I shall lay my head on the asphalt so that the wheels of a car will quickly crush it. When I hear my bones crack I'll say: Take my blood, city, like a scarlet carnation on your weary breast.' 'You are talking like a madman!' They hear the call to prayer and one friend says to the other: 'Let's go and pray.' 'Why should we pray? Perhaps God himself hates us.' The whole city appears to disintegrate around the author in a series of cameos in which citizens complain of life and welcome death. There seems to be no solution to life other than death. Or sleep? The story ends: 'I shall sleep for a hundred years.'

In *Snow at the end of night* (1961) the hero Yusuf is tortured by the problems of family relationships. He is spoilt by his mother and hates his father. He experiences feelings of uselessness and consequently lives in the world of his imagination. It is a world filled with horror – of cats mauling birds, of vipers, smooth and black, of sheep slaughtered on feast days. The daughter has run away from home and dishonoured them. The father urges the son to look for her. 'Find her however you can and cut her throat, bitch that she is.' Yusuf, Hamlet-like, retreats into dreams rather than action. He feels death is near. 'Ferry me across, death, in your boat.' He longs for the viper to strangle him, taking him away from all his family. Finally he dreams that he meets his sister and in a frenzy of revenge and family honour cuts her throat. She dies moaning 'Brother, brother'. He immediately relents and he and his sister, reunited in affection, kiss and embrace, both blaming their father for their troubles. Yusuf then falls into dreamless sleep, presumably satisfied that he has pleased everyone. It is interesting that this negative story was first published in Beirut, awarded a literary prize there, and then reprinted in Damascus in 1978 at the height of the Baath regime.

In *Face of the moon* (Beirut, 1962) Tamir treats another side of human relationships, that of sexual desire in a woman. With great delicacy and psychological insight he deals with a subject that is still very largely taboo in Arab society. A Syrian critic considered this story to be a peak in the development of the modern Syrian short story and marked a move into the stage of its maturity. In subject matter it also makes an interesting comparison with *Snow* where the father took it for granted that the 'erring' girl had no rights herself and deserved death for her actions. In *Face of the moon* there is a recognition that a woman has sexual feelings and a right to express them.

The 1967 war with Israel was a turning point in many writers' lives. It was the beginning of disillusion with politics and politicians and a moving inward to avoid the realities of society and it brought a deep sense of alienation, a cessation of participation in a society to which the writer found it difficult to relate. These feelings are expressed by Tamir in fantasies in which reality and time are broken down, and the individual suffers and feels helpless in face of forces stronger than himself. The alienated self is caught in the maze of his own hallucinations and delusions. Death often marks the end of aimless wanderings in a world devoid of meaning. In *The green tree* (1970), a boy (Talal) and a girl (Randa) meet under a green tree. They fantasize about life and play various roles, queen, thief, beggar, commander. Sometimes they are cruel to each other, sometimes kind. They enjoy living in their world of fantasy in which the girl wishes to become a flower seen only by the sun and sky. Their play is shattered by the arrival of a group of armed men and a prisoner whom they tie to the tree and shoot. The bullets pierce man and tree and both fall to the ground. 'Randa burst into tears as the men went marching away. Then she threw herself towards Talal and pressed her head against his chest. He folded his arms around her and pressed her to him. They thus become one being, trembling, longing to flee. It was not long before they turned into a rock.' It is not necessary to look for a message in this story but the development is clear. Two people live in a world of their imagination which is shattered by the sudden intrusion of violence. They cannot react and only stand and watch as both a life is destroyed and the green tree (comfort, hope, security) is killed. As happens in dreams they try to flee but are turned to stone and unable to move.

The day on which Genghis Khan was angry (1979) is a more straightforward allegorical fable. Genghis Khan, the all-powerful ruler, is walking in the street and meets a donkey who makes fun of him and tells him that it was once a man who was forced to go around on all fours (as a sycophant) in order to gain wealth and prestige. He failed by not being sycophantic enough and became a donkey. 'The best man is the one who is the biggest creep', says the donkey. 'Your answers are not without wit which could make you fit to be one of my ministers', replies Genghis. The donkey answers insolently: 'It is not unusual for Genghis Khan to choose as one of his ministers, someone who was a man and who became a donkey.' This answer annoys Genghis intensely and he orders the donkey's owner to beat it mercilessly – which he does out of fear. Genghis returns to his palace and orders all donkey owners to whip their animals constantly. The humour in this story is refreshing and the political message needs no comment.

In *A summary of what happened to Muhammad al-Mahmudi* (1978) political satire reaches the height of the absurd. The hero of the title spends the days of his retirement sitting in a café reading at his favourite table. When he eventually dies he is buried beneath the table and happily listens to the customers' conversation. Only at night does he feel alone and frightened. One day the police come to dig him up and accuse him of criticizing the actions of the government. Muhammad protests that while he was alive he never once criticized either the government or the rulers. The police reply that he stands condemned out of his own mouth for not having praised the government. 'Does it not in your opinion deserve praise? Even if what you say is true, it's still strange in itself because everybody is corrupt and full of hatred and revenge. They blame the government and rulers and forget their duty to obey those in authority.' Muhammad agrees and says that everyone talks politics these days. At this the policeman takes notice and promises Muhammad immunity if he agrees to become an informer. 'But how can I help when I'm dead?' The policeman laughs and explains. So Muhammad is reburied in the café and spends his days happily and his nights fruitfully – no longer frightened – writing down what he has heard from the customers during the day.

Walid Ikhlasi was born in 1935 in Alexandretta, the Syrian province ceded to Turkey in 1939. The family moved to Aleppo where he has continued to live and work. He is one of the most prolific and versatile of Syrian writers, producing novels, stories and plays. His early years under French colonialism have coloured his life and the questions of oppression, domination and power have had a deep influence on his writings. He has asked: 'Why does the strongest control everything? The question of right arising from power shocked me.' He hated oppression in its various forms and became preoccupied with the issue of national and individual freedom. To preserve his freedom he remained aloof from politics. 'I stopped thinking of joining any political party. I was afraid of losing my intellectual freedom.' 'I am rooted in the idea of freedom and democracy and my life and most of my writings centre around these questions.'[5] As with Tamir, Ikhlasi takes refuge in his writing in symbolism, allegory, surrealism and even the absurd, leaving to the reader (and perhaps the censor) the hard work of interpretation. He considers his search for new forms as an honest pursuit of freedom and a refusal to be tied down to specific literary forms.

Ikhlasi has published some eight collections of short stories which cover a very wide range of topics and approaches. Central to many of them is the plight of man in contemporary society and his search for identity and self-knowledge in an increasingly alien world. He finds himself unable to communicate and in nightmare situations where he is tried for crimes he knows nothing about or where he completely loses his identity. These themes are often treated ambiguously or impressionistically and convey a depressing atmosphere.

In *Crime and punishment* a man is inexplicably in a police station to which he had been taken in a closed car. A soldier says: 'Confess that you are guilty.' The man replies: 'I did not kill anyone.' The soldier shouts roughly: 'Confess that you have broken article 19 of law 140.' The man complains that he knows nothing of any such law. The soldier ignores this and declares that he will count to ten and that the man will confess before he finishes. The terrified man can confess to nothing. The soldier says mockingly: 'Well, citizen, you've proved your bravery.' The scene ends: 'Then a red hot bullet pierced the calm and penetrated flesh and blood. I fell to the ground.' This very short story told with great economy typifies Ikhlasi's view of a pitiless and capricious world in face of which the ordinary citizen is powerless.

In *The nightmare* a man awakes one morning to find that he cannot move from his bed. His hair is fastened to the pillow with small nails. 'I told myself that a nightmare had stayed with me from night until morning.' But he has been imprisoned in his own house, windows and door guarded and telephone cut off. Again the hero of a story cries out that he is innocent but he cannot escape. He shouts from his window: 'You people down there, who will get me out of here?' People turn to him for a moment and then pass by regardless. In this story, in addition to the unexplained imprisonment, there is the inability to communicate with the outside world. Man is cut off from his fellow men and condemned to loneliness.

Ikhlasi touches on the perplexity of identity in other stories, but he does not claim that self-knowledge leads to a solution. In *The mirror* a man is walking fairly contentedly through the streets of a town. 'I was happily caressing the limbs of my body, inwardly sure of their existence and intactness. I had become happy, feeling my fingertips from outside and my skin inside my body, sure of the continuance of my soul and mind and thought.' This must be too good to last? The man begins to dislike the town and hurries away to the rural suburbs. There he finds some cool water and looks into its mirror-like surface. 'I found reflected an ugly face. I closed my eyes a moment and then turned round looking for the intruder. I found no one. After a while I knew that the face was mine and that everything had been fixed in order to rob of me of the happiness which had accompanied me for a long period of my life.' Nothing is certain, nothing can be taken for granted in life and even that which you thought you knew can be deceptive.

In *Where is the obliterated face going?* a man is on urgent business in the town and is trying to find a taxi. None comes and he becomes cold, anxious and angry as all the taxis pass by full up. Eventually one arrives and begins to take the man far too slowly through the town. He begs the driver to hurry but he utters not a word despite being addressed several times. Perhaps he is deaf and dumb. 'I shouted aloud. Can't you hear me?' Eventually the driver turns round. 'I could not master the fear which enveloped me. The driver had no face, just a piece of flesh in which red, yellow and black were mixed, colourless, yet with every colour. I could not bear that horrendous obliterated face to drive me and I opened the door and threw myself on the ground, passing madly along beneath me.' Man's attempts to 'arrive' are fruitless and he is forced through life aimlessly by faceless power.

These stories of alienation are complemented by others in which Ikhlasi demonstrates a positive commitment to nationalism and to the Palestinian cause. He is bitter over the loss of Palestine, particularly after the *naksa* (setback) of 1967, and over French colonialist oppression in Syria and Algeria. One story throws light on his feelings. In *The viper and the days of war* a family lives in an old house in Aleppo during the days of the French occupation. A presumed viper has made its nest in the ceiling of the house and it proves impossible to move it. The family wishes to rid itself of both intruders. Eventually, the Syrians rise up and defeat the occupiers and at the same time the family manages to find the viper and kill it. When they see the disgusting body of the dead snake they realize that it was only a rat after all.

Ikhlasi has written four remarkable novels in addition to his numerous short stories. Their form and style which have broken with more traditional narrative techniques have aroused considerable controversy. Their content is mainly comment on the predicament of man in society. In *The lap of the beautiful lady* the author describes the state of Syrian intellectuals, their alienation and their inability to achieve their aims in a world governed by material values and oppressive forces. He does not consider society alone as responsible for this predicament as man also makes choices which deepen his alienation. In *Sorrows of ashes* the author lays stress on conflict, anxiety, corruption and meaninglessness. In one section the hero migrates from village to town. He dislikes village life, yet the town has dislocated him and created a sense of aimlessness. He feels unable to fight, to change the oppressive nature of society. 'We are trapped in an odious situation.'

The atmosphere of gloom is continued in Ikhlasi's fourth novel

The domesticated colocynth (bitter apple) where he paints a picture
of a world of frustration and repression. Most of the characters
come from socially depressed classes – workers and peasants – and
suffer a life of oppression. The novel treats the loss of ideals with the
characters failing to achieve their aims. The author is condemning
those forces which alienate man from himself and from his freedom
of choice. Man to Ikhlasi is a victim of internal and external forces,
someone whose ideals often fail. His characters try to live up to
them but are too weak and succumb to the evils of the world. They
end up disillusioned or dead – they are driven by faceless forces or
see their real face in the mirror. Yet his message is not entirely
pessimistic. He wants the experience of his heroes to be a lesson or a
message. He has written: 'When a character in my stories dies, his
death is meant to be life to others. His death must encourage us to
cling more to life.'[6]

Among other Syrians writing today there are three women
authors, living and working in Beirut. The best known is Ghada
al-Samman who was born in a Syrian village in 1942. Her father,
from a poor rural family, eventually became head of the University
of Damascus and Minister of Education. She studied English
literature in Damascus and London and left for Beirut in 1964 for
further study. She soon abandoned her formal education to follow
her activities as journalist, poet and novelist. She has published
widely, especially short stories, and has gained a reputation as one
of the most popular of contemporary Arab women writers. She
shares the preoccupations of her male colleagues, identity and loss
of self, detestation of the harsh and unsettling social and economic
condition of the time, the tension between tradition and modernity.
In addition she is alienated by her femininity and her intellect. She
feels marginal, yet too proud to beg for pity. Her heroines share
these attributes. They cannot say what they want to become yet one
thing is certain, their present life nauseates them. They disown the
bourgeoisie to which they belong and which they see as devoted to
folly and sexually infirm, while the humbler citizens know how to
love and find the path to happiness.

Gipsy without a haven by Ghada al-Samman is a monologue
spoken by a woman, lying in bed, to her lover who is apart from her.
He is married and she engaged to be married to a man of whom her
family approves. Her thoughts demonstrate the tearing dilemma
the Middle Eastern woman faces in traditional society, although in
her case the situation is made worse (or impossible) by the fact that

the man she loves is already married. She cannot decide whether to conform to tradition or to break away; she wanders mentally between these two courses of action – a gypsy with no safe haven. One side of her longs to lose her identity completely in that of her lover: 'Your embrace, my haven, how can I escape . . . ? I feel you waking in my veins as you wake every night uniting with me. Your smile is imprinted on my lips, the smoke of your cigarette coming from my mouth.' The other side longs to conform. She knows that whichever course she chooses she cannot be happy. 'I am torn apart like a fabulous animal with two heads, each facing the opposite way.' 'It is a tragedy that we spend our life rushing after a cup because we will die if we have not drunk from it . . . And if we reach it and drink, we also die. In the first case love and longing kill us, the second the lack of love kills. It kills us just to understand ourselves.'

No one can escape the loneliness of self. 'Each of us is in an isolated glass cage. We speak but we do not listen to one another. We spend life wandering in woods, on the shore, amongst the islands where there is no haven, no shelter, and even when a haven appears from afar we know that it is not for us.' She sees quite clearly that she lives a life of deception, wearing a mask that hides her inner self. 'Two men are struggling for her. One wants to give her a home. Her mask loves the home and she wears it in order to bring a smile to the faces of those she loves . . . The other man only has for her a new tale of wandering. And she is content with that because a home is accidental and exile and sadness are the reality of human existence now.' And yet her traditional self still wishes to please her family: 'Perhaps it is my mask which ties me to them . . . the mask of a well-brought up girl which has become part of my face. If I pulled it off would anything remain underneath?' Her conclusion is gloomy enough: 'I am a wandering gipsy . . . weeping for a lost haven, for the roads we are forced to travel and for the strangers I accompany through life's journey, simulating happiness and joy in meeting them.'

In *Widow of the wedding feast* Ghada al-Samman treats a rather similar subject, the narrator's love for a married man. It is all seen as a repeated dream or nightmare, but she asks: 'Yet what is reality? What is a dream? I no longer know.' The story deals with a relationship that cannot be consummated because of social conditions and the taboos of tradition. In addition, the author bitterly attacks the mores of those around her, those who stultify her life and whom she calls 'the gang of the bourgeois mafia'. Her mother, a member of this gang 'tried to make me grow up as a model of her and to erase from my system any madness I may have inherited from my father, the poet, and to change the gypsy blood in my veins into blue blood befitting a future lady of society who does not dream'. She asks her lover how he managed to change her from 'something calm and settled' into a 'severed artery'. Unfortunately, the change is too much and her dream of happiness becomes a nightmare. When she eventually goes to the house of her lover, his wife tells her that he has had a nervous breakdown. Her dream is over and destroyed. 'I collapse and dig my nails into the ashes and gaze stunned at the dream that has awakened me and walked away, passed by and committed suicide.'

These nightmares becomes more intense and more explicit as the author lives through the civil war in Beirut. She has devoted a whole work to this period entitled *Beirut nightmares* (1975). She describes her life amid the fighting and destruction and how it has changed her attitudes. The war has once and for all shown up the hollow values of the bourgeoisie which she so bitterly criticized and, yet, she now sees some hope. Surely, nothing can be worse than the slaughter and suffering of the present. Surely, the future must be different, if not better. The time has come to defy death by living more fully. It is this call for life which distinguishes her later work. 'No longer is tomorrow dreaded as a dull repetition of today . . . For now tomorrow is ever different, bringing the hope for some of peace and order, for others of danger and excitement.'[7] Whether after another ten years' fighting and of hopes dashed she still feels the same it is difficult to know.

Ghada al-Samman, a Syrian, is living through the trials of the Lebanese and of the Arabs in Beirut. Halim Barakat is a Syrian who has written novels about events outside his country, the Palestinian-Israeli confrontation. He was born in a Syrian village near the Lebanese border, of Christian Orthodox parents who soon moved to Lebanon. In a way his birthplace is irrelevant as he writes as an Arab about Arab problems. He was educated at the American University in Beirut where he teaches as a sociologist. He began to write fiction in the 1950s and concentrated particularly on the fate of Palestinian refugees. As a sociologist he is interested in the problems posed by exile and the strains on those whose lives have been uprooted. His novel, *Six days* (1961), describes the efforts of a Palestinian village to defend itself against the Israelis in 1948 over a six-day period. The work has some merits as a novel but the author devotes a substantial part of it to criticizing Arab society and to commenting on its faults, its traditionalism and the feeling of alienation among the young. The title seems particularly apt, prophetic of the coming (and worse) six-day war with Israel in 1967 and of the six days of the creation which are picked up in Barakat's later novel, *The return of the Flying Dutchman to the sea.* In it he chronicles the events of the war as seen through the eyes of several characters and comments on Arab politics and society in general. The Dutchman figure represents Palestine, like 'a ship sailing aimlessly across the seas of terror and ignorance for a long period and unable to dock anywhere'. The author vividly describes the atmosphere of expectation of victory just before the war began, expectations so bitterly shattered. 'All Arab public opinion was in support of that action [blocking the Straits of Tiran] and that feeble word support is incapable of translating the deep emotion that had invaded the Arab world . . . The Arabs were full of triumph.' Some characters are more apprehensive and criticize Arab governments for their inefficiency. 'Look at our institutions. Look at our parties. They do nothing. We are quite ignorant about organization and working as a team . . . We are living in a past age.' The six days of the action of the war and of the novel match the six days of creation. The first day is 'the threshold' or the beginning. 'Earth is deserted and empty and there is darkness over the deep. The spirit of God does not move over the sea.' There seems to be nothing for the Palestinians. Hope comes as the promise of return in 1967 and is quickly extinguished – in six short days. The last day is the first of 'many days of dust', not the seventh on which God rested and saw that all was good. 'On the seventh day the Arab did not rest. His seventh day will last, alas, more than a single day. He has no idea how long into the future it will last. A long time? Months? Years? All that the Arab created in the first six days was dust. Darkness returns to cover earth . . . The Arab saw everything that he had made and behold it was very bad.' In the end nothing has changed for the better. 'The flying Dutchman returned to the sea while still longing for the shore. How could he remain exiled and rootless for ever?' Thus ends this powerful evocation of the Palestinian tragedy. Barakat's novel remains one of the most telling commentaries on the 1967 *naksa* and its implications.

Drama

Drama first appeared in Syria as early as the mid-nineteenth century but did not begin to flourish until a hundred years later. In the early 1960s the Ministry of Culture established and subsidized official theatres, the National Theatre in Damascus, the Itinerant Theatre, the People's Theatre in Aleppo, in which the actors, designers, producers are salaried government employees. In addition the government has sponsored an annual theatre festival in Damascus during which groups from the Arab world and Europe present plays and hold workshops on recent theatrical developments. The Ministry of Culture has also sponsored prizes for dramatists and has established a publishing house for their work. This sponsorship has its disadvantages. The ministry determines which plays will be staged and, in the first fifteen years of its existence, of 54 plays produced by the National Theatre only 7 were by Syrian authors. The government may fear the impact of criticism inherent in certain writing as a play publicly performed before an audience can have an immediate effect on the large group of people gathered together at one time with a shared knowledge of political and social conditions. In this way a play has more impact than the most critical short story. Nevertheless, official support of the theatre has encouraged several Syrian authors to write on many themes. Different forms have been tried from poetic drama to surrealism and the theatre of the absurd. Many contain social criticism of outdated traditions, of the position of women, of poverty and exploitation, of the rottenness of government and the prevalence of bribery. A prime example of the irony of government sponsorship of drama is provided by the works of Ali Aqla Irsan who has been director of the National Theatre. His play *Prisoner 95* (1972) criticizes Arab rulers and systems for keeping the masses trapped in their poverty. 'The victor, whatever he may be, will be the new jailer and will buy more efficient locks'; and in *Caesar's pleasure* (1975) he examines the relationship between the state and the writer. To avoid direct criticisms the action is set in Roman times and describes the delicate relationship between the playright, Plautus, and his ruler, Caesar. A play about the slaves of Rome arouses Caesar's anger and he orders the arrest of the author. The latter to escape imprisonment agrees to work for Caesar.

Of the many plays written since the 1960s three may be singled out as typifying certain themes and trends. Walid Ikhlasi, in addition to his short stories and novels, has written a number of plays in which he deals with human issues which go beyond the local socio-political context, themes therefore of universal validity. They also demonstrate his continual experimentation with different dramatic techniques. In *Pleasure 21* (1965) man's predicament, particularly in face of the development of modern technology, is the central theme. The play is set against an unidentified background and the characters are unnamed symbols – a beautiful woman, a physician, a gay waiter, a depressed man and so on – to give the play a more than local validity. It is written in the manner of the theatre of the absurd, full of bizarre incidents and seemingly inconsequential dialogue. The author criticizes the West with its apparently superior technology and its obsession with material gain for exploiting the underprivileged masses. The characters in the play have no purpose in life and no genuine human feelings; they only try to gratify their own selfish needs – hence the title of the play and the place of the action – Pleasure Club 21. Pleasure is all and sought by all even amidst pervading death and decay. Several characters represent or speak for certain abstract concepts – the physician for science, the old woman (owner of a coffin factory!) for capitalism, the black man kept in a cage for the oppressed masses, a beautiful woman who represents some sort of escape. The physician, who is held responsible for the thoughtless development of technology, believes that science is the solution for all ills. A newcomer rushes on to the stage and announces that the wind of death is approaching and that everyone should run away. The scientist is sceptical: 'The experiment has succeeded, failure is damned. I have killed it.' The newcomer retorts that death spares no one. The old woman thinks that science can stop the wind, but a feeling of gloom pervades the characters and even the scientist begins to doubt whether he can really stop it: 'I did not think of the wind', and in the end he admits defeat. 'I was thinking of establishing a new way of life. I have failed. Now the end begins and I have done nothing of any value, have I? I know that I haven't.' A depressed man comments: 'But you have created death of the highest perfection!' The old woman believes that money can solve all problems and offers to buy the scientist's invention: 'I will pay a lot for this secret.' She agrees to sign a contract for its purchase and the five of them plan to experiment with it upon others. 'How many people can it kill in an hour?' she asks eagerly, thinking of an increase in the coffin trade. She later becomes frightened at the thought of death and collapses on the stage.

According to the playright, part of the pleasure of life is watching others suffer and the black man in the cage has been trained to perform at the crack of a whip. He cries in pain each time it is wielded by his trainer. The others urge him to perform more until he eventually revolts and strangles his trainer. The beautiful woman opens his cage and allows him to escape. 'Don't release him', cries the depressed man, 'There is no hope anymore.' But in a final burst of optimism the woman determines to escape together with the black man: 'I can't stand the sight of this graveyard anymore . . . We are leaving . . . The wind of death has missed us. The blood is running in our veins. I am so happy.' She and the black man exit leaving the depressed man behind weeping a while. The slave has freed himself and the woman abandons those in the Pleasure Club – signalling a revolt against oppression and a search for better conditions in a society free from destructive science and social tyranny.

Muhammad Maghut is a Syrian (born 1934), known both for his poetry and his plays. He also writes for television which brings his work to a very wide audience. He is a witty writer and provides scripts for Syria's leading comedian. His play *The hunchback Sparrow* was written in 1967 and does not appear yet to have been performed. It is a surrealist vision of a nightmare world of suffering and persecution, often difficult to grasp but powerful in its overall effect. It is a savage indictment of the totalitarian state and mocks many of its institutions, the law, the ruler, the bureaucracy. It is hard to believe that if Syrian rulers ever took the play as a direct attack upon themselves they would allow it to be performed, and it was in fact published in Beirut. It opens in a desert prison camp in an atmosphere of gloom and despair. The prisoners include a dwarf, an old man and a bachelor. An unknown voice explains why they are imprisoned. 'Brothers, you are here because the others are there . . . You are here because God does not sit under the jasmine or in the perforations of guitars, but in the mouths of guns and on the wounds of captives.' The prisoners discuss their conditions and the way they have been tortured and they occasionally complain. On each such occasion the gaoler rushes in shouting: 'Who's slandering the state?' and threatens further punishment. The prisoners long for a normal life and the old man who seems to represent hope and humanity in a dehumanized society sighs: 'Ah, your talk has reminded me of water. It's marvellous for a man to remember something useful, something silent and well behaved in this cursed time. I'm dying of thirst. All I long for at this very moment is to kiss every unhappy person in the world, every deformed person, every sad one, and then die immediately before my saliva has dried on their wounds and their moustaches.' The other prisoners mock him but soon relent and ask him to forgive them. He replies: 'Let what we have said go with the wind. Let's consider it just a fleeting rebuke on board a ship which is preparing to set sail. Let us from now on and forever bend our efforts and our desires towards lowly and affectionate things, for the sake of grass and birds.'

The gaoler rushes in shouting: 'Who's slandering the state?' The next scene continues in the prison camp with the prisoners discussing their fate. A student, still young, sees a ray of hope and says to a shoemaker: 'I don't exactly know what I am because a man in this kind of place loses his individuality. While you others were talking, plunged up to your ears in a world dominated by gunpowder, hate and pallor, I caught sight of a green leaf through the window.' The shoemaker however has little hope left. He does not know why he was thrown into prison: 'I was working as a shoemaker . . . when some youths came in . . . and hung up a picture of some heroes or other. I didn't stop them. Then some other youths came in and hung up a picture of some other heroes. I didn't stop them . . . Then after an hour or maybe millions of hours I found myself soaked in blood and heard shouts: Sign here. No here. No there. And I was screaming, weeping, beseeching. *Student*: Did you scream during the interrogation? *Shoemaker*: Good God was I singing? *Student*: Great. *Shoemaker*: Who's great? *Student*: Screaming is. Do you like screaming? I adore it. Do you adore anything else? Nothing else. In that case you are a nationalist!' The prison scene ends with the gaoler (or the government) having a change of heart and ordering the prisoners to dress their wounds, wipe away their bruises, in readiness for their release.

The second act is set in front of delapidated and dirty peasant houses and gives the characters, mainly peasants, the opportunity to discuss their wretched state and the indifference of the government. They are awaiting the Agricultural Commissioner who they hope will help to solve their problems. At last he arrives. '*Boy*: The Commissioner has arrived. *All*: Where is he? *Boy*: He's come and gone. *Grandmother*: Come and gone? What did he do then, by all the devils. *Boy*: Nothing. Nothing. He put his head out of his car window, looking at the first field he came to, glanced at it as he would his watch, then he set off home yawning.' An Industrial Commissioner arrives and is only concerned to lecture them. 'Dear people, we have heard from students returning from holiday that certain discontented old men and women here and there are complaining that the authorities do not help them enough and know nothing of their dried up fields and starving fowls. The authorities absolutely deny such contemptible feelings and declare that heaven alone bears responsibility for such trivial creatures . . . Weep, weep, as long as you like. We never care as long as the time of sad songs is past and the time of waiting amongst the springs is over.' The Commissioner ignores their complaints and leaves the villagers feeling insulted, hurt and ignored.

The third act is the most ironic in the play. It is set in a sumptious marble palace amongst leafy trees. The idealistic old man who was a prisoner in the desert has now become absolute ruler, corrupted by power. His ideals forgotten, he is indifferent to the needs of his people who are clamouring for food. 'Tell them to eat their fowls or their children.' A dwarf who had also once been a prisoner pleads with the ruler. 'We knew you, nameless old man, and therefore we have come to you with wide open hearts. You wept over a bird that flew away . . . Now you are here with the same eyes, lips and hands, standing behind fortified walls to spit your hate at us like a spring.' The ruler will have nothing to do with him or the rest of the people who revolt him. In theory they are all right, 'But face to face you hear their moaning and groaning. You see a few inches away their sores and their teeth and their filth as thick as the bark on a tree. This is what makes me shun them and the whole world like a bird who is wary of the bullet . . . I have seen the people in far off prison camps praying like monks for the fatherland and fighting each other with chains over a scrap of pickle.' Addressing the people he invites them all to go to hell: 'All that matters is that the fatherland survives.' The people shout back, calling for love and rain, asking to be treated with dignity. The dwarf calls the ruler a coward, a monster who is ruining the whole nation and degrading dignity and liberty. The infuriated ruler orders him to be shot before he says anything more. As he dies the ruler's servants murmurs: 'Others will only say it, sire.'

The final act is a horrific climax, a Kafka-like trial scene. The man on trial is the shoemaker, accused of calling out for rainfall and love. The judge shows him a file in which his life is recorded. 'What you do not know at all is that your whole life is written down in this file and that our justice does not sit on rooftops so that you can predict its results. This is clear from your eyes. No, our justice is hidden and reveals itself when it wishes, but only as much as is necessary for the welfare of the state and the safety of its citizens.' The shoemaker is accused by the judge of not complying with the policy of the state. 'The accused was seen in the company of a woman of dark skin in torn clothing together with a number of children, walking leisurely beneath a lightly clouded sky in a manner not consistent with the firmness and glory demanded by his fatherland.' The shoemaker begs for mercy but the judge in a long speech explains that mistakes have been made in the past which must not be allowed to happen again even if many people have to suffer. 'We shall cleave through the waves of the world with the knife of liquidation between our teeth.' The accused is to be held in the Central Liberty Prison and then hanged. His two innocent children are also condemned through association with their father. They are too young to hang and therefore are to be shot with 'small bore' rifles. The scene ends in horror as the two children are tied to a post and shot.

An evening party for the 5th of June (1971) is by Syria's leading dramatist, Saadallah Wannus. He was born in northern Syria in 1941 and educated in Syria, Cairo and at the Theatrical Institute in the Sorbonne in Paris. He has been employed by the Ministry of Culture and has worked as editor of one of its journals. He has written a number of plays which have been produced with success, both within and outside Syria. He has tried to make his work 'relevant' to the contemporary political and social situation and to make it accessible to the masses. He calls this method of writing the 'politicization' of the theatre and claims that 'The theatre was originally political and still is. Even when it ostensibly avoids political issues it still serves a political object, that is, preventing the masses from being concerned about their problems and preventing them from changing their conditions.' Wannus' objective, therefore, is to create theatre which 'changes, develops, and deepens a collective consciousness of the historical process'[8] and consequently makes the masses aware of their condition and aware of their power to change it. Wannus wishes the audience (the public, or eventually the masses) to participate in his dramas (in itself not a new idea) and to remove the barrier between auditorium and stage. He believes that real interaction cannot take place unless 'the audience, its social class, its cultural conditions, its problems and suffering are defined'.[9] When a play deals with a problem of particular class, unity between actors and audience can be achieved. He wants his plays to be events which move or shock the audience, in which there is communication between public and players, through improvisation and participation.

In addition to dealing with long-term problems, the crisis of the 1967 defeat had its effect on Wannus. The *Evening party* was inspired by the war and is an attempt to instil its lessons into the consciousness of the audience. The problem is stated explicitly in the published edition of the play. 'In the period of setback when people have only two choices – armed resistance or surrender – the task of the theatre is difficult, yet nevertheless clear. It must break with its roots and incorporate the stage and the auditorium into a conscious awakening which must penetrate into the most distant halls of the theatre, into the streets and houses, into the front line, evolving as it spreads into protest, resistance and a clear vision of the future. In this period the theatre betrays its public if it hides the truth; it misleads them if it does not know the truth . . . An *Evening party* is a serious attempt to take on the difficult, yet clear task of a theatre whose rays spontaneously illumine truth and not deception, resistance and not surrender.'

The play marked a turning point in Wannus' career and was an instant success. It puts into practice some of his ideas. The whole theatre becomes the stage and the subtitle states that in this play 'The public, history and officials participate in addition to professional actors'. The form of the drama is ostensibly that of a play within a play although the inner play never takes place. The performance begins with the audience awaiting the beginning of their inner play, which is to deal with the effects of 1967 in a Syrian village. There is a delay and members of the audience become restive, shouting and whistling: 'What a farce. Is this a hotel or a theatre? Perhaps there is a crisis back stage? Perhaps the actors have lost their parts? It's contempt for the audience anyway.' The atmosphere is tense until the producer comes on stage to explain his difficulties in putting on the play as the author has failed to write it. The author himself steps from the audience to discuss what kind of play he should write. A member of the audience shouts out that the director's ideas do not reflect reality. He replies that he wants to produce a dramatic work not a documentary account. However, reality will not go away. As a group of villagers on stage act out a discussion of the events of the war in their village some peasants in the audience rise and complain that this dramatic portrayal does not at all reflect reality. They then describe what really happened. The producer feels that he is losing control of the situation and that matters are going too far. Finally, another member of the audience named 'the official man' gets up and orders the theatre doors to be guarded. The audience is now very eager to hear the truth of what happened in the village and listen angrily to stories of the breakdown of authority and communication. The producer becomes worried about official reaction to these stories. 'Where's all this leading? Where? Has the theatre become a public square? Have you forgotten where you are? You go from one piece of impudence to another. You all want to vomit your brains up in front of us. We are not here for an exhibition of brains and muscles.'

The audience is not at all cowed by the producer's words and they go on to claim that they have their rights and that they should be treated with dignity and be allowed to make criticisms if necessary. The debate is pursued with great vigour until a man in the front row wearing an official uniform gets up shouting: 'Enough all of you. Stop. Let all this stop. Do you think then that discipline has come to an end and that the country has become anarchy?' Immediately order is restored. The audience flatter him as 'Your excellency, your honour, Mr President' and whisper among themselves: 'We warned them of the consequences. Have we forgotten where we live? Damned seductiveness of the tongue.' The official then delivers a political speech glorifying the people, the leader, their achievements, and the whole audience is marched out under arrest, muttering: 'What an evening; let's admit they're heroes; I was sure the end would be sad; we've never seen in all our lives anything like this evening. God curse the theatre and its difficulties.'

The play with its strongly critical tone caused much comment and was seen almost as an event in itself in the aftermath of the 1967 war. Wannus commented: 'As far as I'm concerned it was not a theatrical work. It was, rather, an adventure in a defeated land which was exposed to this severe historical shock.'

Poetry

Whereas the novel and drama were introduced relatively recently into the Arab world under Western influence, poetry is an indigenous form which has flourished from pre-Islamic days. Public recital of odes was a feature of Bedouin life and the public reading of poetry still continues to be part of Arab life. It has also become a much more private art which expresses the deepest personal feelings. Many of the Arab poets who led innovating trends in this century were Egyptian. In later years others have taken up the running, Iraqis, Syrians, Lebanese and Palestinians. Lebanon has been a centre of the avant-garde and the experimental and its effect has spread throughout the Arabic-speaking world. The Syrian poet, Adunis, has had especially wide influence.

Ali Ahmad Said was born in 1930 in Syria and attended secondary school in Latakia. At school he was active in politics and organized demonstrations against the French occupying troops. He was a member of the Syrian National Party of Antun Saada and was influenced in his early days by its ideology of Syrian nationalism, national loyalty and rebirth. He probably took his pen name about this time, Adunis, the mythical god of Syria, a god of nature whose death and return to life represent the decay of nature in winter and its revival in spring. The symbolism in the choice of the name is that of rebirth and resurrection. In 1950 he entered Damascus University and began writing poems which questioned both traditional literary conventions and the social and political structure of Syria. He was imprisoned for his activities and exiled to Beirut in 1956. He took Lebanese nationality and remained there some thirty years, active as editor and writer.[10] He helped to found two very influential literary journals, *Shir* (poetry) and in 1968 *Mawaqif* (positions) which have been vehicles for experimental poetry.

In his writings Adunis has maintained that only radical change in all aspects of life will bring the Arabs into the twentieth century. Then will they be in a position to make a contribution to the advancement of world civilization and of humanity. This means bringing into play all the positive aspects of the Arab heritage and then linking them to positive aspects of other civilizations. To him poetry is a means of inducing revolutionary change and of creating a new society. The poet is the revolutionary hero who will lead his people into a new world, no longer a passive romantic sufferer but the active redeemer. Adunis gradually abandoned the Syrian nationalism of Saada and embraced the Arab cause. He wrote in 1971: 'Arab existence and Arab destiny constitute my reality, not only as a poet, but as a man . . . We have no identity outside the Arab identity.'[11] In his search for revolutionary change and revolutionary poetry Adunis has written works that are not always easy to understand. He uses language which is allusive, evocative and mystical and he even attempts to create a new poetic language. It is difficult to quote briefly from him, taking passages out of context which may only deepen misunderstanding.

His early poems deal with themes of childhood, poverty and death and he remembers with affection his own childhood days and the people of his village. He sees in death merely the start of a new life as it is reunion with earth. This theme and that of resurrection are clearly expressed in his poem *The wanderer*.

> Wanderer – I pray to my dust
> I sing to my soul of exile
> And to a miracle which is not yet complete
> I cross a world which
> My songs burn, and I reach out to the threshold

Together with the poet's redemption will come that of his country. In the powerful poem *Emptiness* (written in Damascus in 1954 when he was taking part in political action), after a bitter attack on modern Arab society Adunis sees some hope for the future of his country.

> The young of my country are shining candles
> We ask one another; where, where is the destruction of emptiness,
>   the wreck of transgression
> And how does it burn to ashes in their face on the dawn of happiness
> And relaxes its mourning for them
> And extinguishes the light of the bright candles
> The young of my country are singing to us their innocent songs
> Saying: In our country is revolution
> Which will create anew the life of the coming morrow
> And open our eyes to a glorious time
> They say: Transgression is dying in our land
> Those who commit transgression are dying
> Emptiness is dying

This vision of a better future is also expressed in another poem by Adunis, *I said to you*, written in a lyrical vein.

> I said to you: 'I have listened to the seas
> Reciting their poems to me. I have listened
> To the ringing sleeping in the shells'
> I said to you: 'I have sung
> At the devil's wedding, at the feast of fairy tales'

> I said to you: 'I saw
> In the rain of history, in the brilliance of the distance
> A fairy and a house'
> Because I cross the seas in my eyes
> I said to you: 'I saw everything
> At the first step from afar'.

But change will not come about easily. It will have to be struggled for and the poet must participate in the struggle. In *You have no choice* he asks:

> What? you will destroy the face of the earth
> You will trace another new face
>
> What then for you will have no choice
> Other than the way of fire
> The torment of refusal
> When the earth becomes either a dumb guillotine or a god

The poet sees his life and his struggle as resembling that of Noah in his ark. In *New Noah* he writes:

> We sailed in the ark. Our oars
> A promise from God under the rain
> And mud . . .
> O Lord, why did you save just us
> Amongst all men and beings?
> Where will you cast us up, on another shore
> Or in our original homeland
> Amongst leaves of death or the wind of life?

The ark must continue to sail, however, searching for a new life and a new god.

> Our appointment is death
> Our shores a despair we are used to
> A frozen sea of iron water we are content with
> We cross it moving to its end
> We move across and do not listen to that God
> We long for another new lord

The events of 1967 and the endless fighting in Lebanon have had a deep effect on Adunis. As the situation worsened so his language becomes more broken and allusive, his images more remote. His ideas are expressed in taut phrases which seem to bear the tension and terror of the moment. In *A mirror for Beirut* (1967) he writes:

> The street is a woman
> Who when grieved recites the Koran
> Or makes the sign of the cross
> Under her breast; night
> Hunchbacked, alien
> Packs his bag
> The silvery wailing dogs
> And the extinguished stars . . .
> In the cellars
> History is inscribed like a coffin
>
> And in the groan of a star or of a dying nation
> Men, women and children sleep
> Without trousers
> Without covering . . .

In a long poem, *The desert*, written during the siege of Beirut by the Israelis in 1982–3 the full horror of the situation is vividly portrayed.

> My time tells me clearly
> You are not part of me
> I say clearly: I am not part of you. I try to understand it
> For I am now a shadow
> Roaming in a forest
> Inside the skull . . .
> There is a stone under my head
> All I said about my life and its death
> Recurs in the silence . . .
> The killing has changed the shape of the city – this rock is of bone
> This smoke the panting of people
> We no longer meet
> There is nothing between us but rejection and exile
> Promises have died, space has died
> Death alone has become a meeting

Adunis asks whether this is the end, whether death is the only future. He is not certain. He asks: 'Do I contradict myself?' and answers: 'You do.' The final question is posed, the final glimmer of hope remains:

He has died. Do I mourn him?
What should I say? That your life was a word, your death its meaning?
Or should I say: The way to the light begins in the forest of darkness?

Nizar Qabbani was born in 1925 in Damascus. He studied law and joined the diplomatic service, working in China, Europe and the Middle East. He resigned in order to found his own publishing house in Beirut. He has gained widespread popularity in the Arab world through his love poetry in which he gives expression to his feelings for women in poems of immediate appeal. His early poetry seemed to express his sexual frustration but as he slowly matured he began to write with more refinement and awareness, still on the subject of women. Events and conditions in the Arab world started to take their toll and in his later poetry he deals with pressing social and political issues, particularly in his collection *In the margin of the book of defeat* (post 1967) where he roundly condemns the Arab leadership. An example of his love poetry is *A short love letter*:

> My darling
> I have much, very much to say
> Where my precious shall I begin?
> Everything in you is a prince . . . a prince
> You who make silk cocoons of my words
> These are my songs . . . this is me
> And this small book contains us . . .
>   What would the earth have become
> If you had not been, if your eyes had not been
> What would it have become?

Or in a slightly more cynical vein, *You want*:

> You want like all women
> The treasures of Solomon
> Like all women, pools of perfume
> Combs of ivory
> And a bevy of slave girls
> You want a lord
> Who praises your name like a parrot
> Saying: I love you, in the morning
> Saying: I love you, in the evening
> Who washes your feet in wine

But now, you Sheherazade of women
I am a workman from Damascus . . . rather poor
My bread I dip in blood
My feelings are modest
My wages modest . . .
I dream of love like others
And of a wife who sews the holes in my clothes
And of a child who sleeps on my knee . . .
You, like all women, want . . .
The eighth wonder.
I have only my pride

Or in the even more cynical *Pregnant*, of sex without love:

Don't turn pale
It's just a hurried word
I feel that I am pregnant
You shouted at me as though you were stung
Never!
We'll tear the child apart
You wanted to throw me out
And began to curse me
Nothing surprises me
For I always knew that you were despicable . . .
You sowed disgrace in my loins
And broke my heart . . .

This feeling of bitterness about relations between the sexes has often been carried over into other poems dealing more generally with society and its problems. In a well-known poem, *Bread, hashish and moon*, he pours scorn on a society that lives on its dreams and drugs.

What does a disc of light do to my country?
To the land of prophets and simpletons
Chewing tobacco and trading in drugs?
What does the moon do to us?
So we lose our pride
And live to beg from heaven
What is in heaven for the lazy and weak?
Who turns to dead men when the moon lives? . . .
On those eastern nights when
The moon becomes full

The East is stripped of all its honour
And fight
The millions who go barefoot
Who believe in four wives
Who meet bread
Only in their imagination
Who live at night in houses of coughing
Who have never seen medicine
They fall down like corpses beneath the light

This despair and bitterness reach a climax in a remarkable poem *Love and petrol* written in 1961 long before the real oil boom. It is a severe criticism of the behaviour of oil-rich Arabs.

When will you understand, sir
That I am not one like your other girl friends
Nor a female conquest to add to your others
Nor a number to be entered in your records . . .
When will you understand
That you won't drug me with your wealth and princedoms
Nor possess the world with your oil and your concessions . . .
Wallow, oil prince in the mud of your pleasures
Like an old rag . . . wallow in your errors
You've got petrol . . . so squeeze it on the feet of your girl friends
In the night clubs of Paris . . . for you have killed your sense of honour
At the feet of the whores there . . . you have buried your treasures
You have sold Jerusalem, you have sold God, you have sold the ashes
    of your dead
Jerusalem sinks in its blood
While you, victim of your lusts,
Sleep . . . as though the tragedy is not part of your tragedy
When will you understand?
When will the human being within you awake?

Muhammad Maghut is also a prolific poet and has experimented in his poetry in a way similar to that in his dramatic works. He experiments with language and images, uses paradox, seeming *non sequiturs*, sometimes to the despair of more traditional critics. His overriding concern is with human suffering, injustice and with the question whether there can ever be any redress, whether the hungry, the imprisoned, the poor will ever be able to escape their plight, whether prayers are heard in heaven. These feelings are expressed in two poems in a collection aptly titled *Joy is not my calling*; first in *From the threshhold to heaven*:

Now
As sad rain
Wets my sad face
I dream of a ladder of dust
Of hunched backs
And hands pressed on knees
To climb to highest heaven
To know
Where our sighs and prayers go
Oh my love
All the sighs and prayers
All the cries and calls for help
Coming from millions of lips and hearts
And across thousands of years and centuries
Must be gathered together somewhere in heaven like clouds
And perhaps my words now
Are near to the words of Jesus
So let us wait for heaven to weep
My love

And a similar theme is pursued in *The postman's fear*:

Prisoners in every place
Send me all your
Terror and wailing and grief
Fisherman on every shore
Send me all your
Empty nets and seasickness
Peasants on every land
Send me all your
Flowers and threadbare rags
With all the breasts which are torn
And stomachs ripped open
And nails pulled out
To my address . . . in any cafe
In any street in the world
I am preparing an enormous file
On human suffering
To send to God
As soon as it is signed by the lips of the hungry
And the eyelashes of those who are waiting
But you wretched ones everywhere
What I fear most
Is that God may be illiterate

Radio, Television, Films

Published literature and the theatre reach relatively small audiences. The cinema, radio and television are means of offering
culture, entertainment and information to the masses. The spoken
word presents no problem to the semi-literate or illiterate listener,
particularly if it is in Syrian dialect as opposed to the classical
literary Arabic of theatre and novel; radios are relatively cheap and
cinema and television screens can be provided by the government.
Centrally directed states consider control of the media essential to
the development of their policies in spreading propaganda and the
official view of events. They can also be used to propagate
education and to introduce new ideas and techniques into the
remotest parts of the country. Syrian radio broadcasts news, drama,
political and other interviews and even music to support the Baath
party and President Asad. Radio comes first in terms of numbers of
listeners, some two million sets, followed by television viewers,
some half million sets, and newspaper readers. National radio
coverage of the country is complete. There is one main radio
programme supplemented by the Voice of the People, a more
recent venture designed for a less sophisticated audience.

Television offers more direct entertainment and education than
radio. It made its debut in 1960 during the union with Egypt and has
been developing slowly since that time. There is one national
channel which broadcasts news and political programmes which
attempt to explain the thinking of the Syrian leaders and their
policies. News broadcasts are the most important programme for
keeping the activities of the president and party before the viewers.
News items and guidance over programme contents are supplied to
television by the Syrian Arab News Agency. Both television and
radio are financed by the government and the Directorate of
Broadcasting is part of the Ministry of Information. Perhaps
surprisingly there is some advertising on television although it is
reported that the ministry is not very enthusiastic about it. The
commercials are often from state-run industries, shoes, soap,
clothing and so on, although others are beginning to appear for
foreign imported goods. Syrian authors are eager to write for
television as it reaches such a wide audience, despite the stricter
control over what they are allowed to write than there is for the
theatre. Some writers, therefore produce scripts for other Arab
television services where there is less censorship. Imported pro-

grammes for Syrian television come from Egypt (whose serials and plays are popular) and Eastern Europe, less from the West as their content is not always considered suitable for Syrian audiences.

The Syrian cinema industry is not large and other Arab countries, particularly Egypt and Algeria, have a greater production. The first film was shown in Aleppo in 1908 and the first locally produced one in 1928 in Damascus. Entitled *The innocent victim* its plot was influenced by the type of gangland adventures favoured in Hollywood. It was a private initiative and was followed by another in 1937 on the Arab revolt in Palestine, an interesting venture which included documentary scenes from foreign films. At the same time another producer was shooting news reels. Despite these early attempts no industry was established with capital backing and modern equipment.

After the Second World War a group of Syrian businessmen founded a film company which produced a film in Egypt in the late 1940s entitled *Princess Laila*. According to a Syrian film critic[12] the producer of this film was responsible for making it 'a complete failure'. The company had been able to obtain finance for its activities but did not have the essential experience. Other individuals were at the same time trying rather unsuccessfully to produce feature and documentary films, notably one on the *Syrian army battle* in 1949. From then until 1961 according to the same critic: 'Ten empty years passed' and 'the existence of a Syrian cinema was almost forgotten'. During the years of the United Arab Republic, Syria adopted certain Egyptian institutions such as a Ministry of Culture which had a section devoted to the cinema. When the Baathis took over they immediately began to encourage the cinema and established the National Film Organization which made several short documentary films and sent technicians to study abroad. At the same time the private sector has been producing its own films, several of which have had more than local success. These have often had a certain propaganda tendency – the triumph of Arab nationalism, historical fiction glorifying the past or films depicting the ills of life under the French occupation or previous Syrian regimes. Palestine has also been popular as a subject, as a symbol of resistance and as a demonstration of the refusal to accept defeat. The work of the Palestinian writer, Ghassan Kanafani, has provided scripts for three films, notably his novel *Men in the sun* (1972) filmed under the titled *The deceived* – the story of three Palestinians who, in order to enter Kuwait secretly, use the services of a tanker lorry driver to take them across the frontier. He hides them in the empty tank of the lorry which he leaves parked in the sun at the frontier crossing. The three die from the intense heat. This film, produced in Syria by an Egyptian, was intended to jolt the public into an awareness of the justice of the Palestinian cause and of the ease with which it can be abused or manipulated.

A few films have dealt with contemporary Syrian life and conditions. A leading director, Umar Amiralay, produced a well-received film *Daily life in a Syrian village* (1974) which was shot in the eastern region of the country. The producer worked with Saadallah Wannus to produce a work which showed with sympathy yet openly the problems of rural life, its hardship, corruption and humanity. It has been hailed as the best Arab film ever to deal with this kind of subject. It is intended to be part of a much larger study of Syrian society in general. In 1976 the same director made a film *The hens* which has been shown abroad, also dealing slightly satirically with Syrian village life.

Samir Zikra is a writer director who after an education in Damascus studied in the Moscow film school from which he graudated in 1973. On his return to Syria he served in the army and worked in its film department during the 1973 war. He made documentaries such as *We will never forget* and *The witnesses*. A recent film of his, *The half-metre incident*, however, sharply satirizes Syrian bureaucracy and the difficulties of falling in love. It is set in Damascus in June 1967 and the hero is a government tax official whose world revolves around his office and home. He has never had much success in affairs of the heart and the film tells of his unsuccessful attempt to court Nada. This film of ironic social criticism interweaves love and politics and questions received ideas of morality and marriage and established ideas about war. As it is set in June 1967 the radio daily announces Syrian victories only finally to have to admit defeat. The hero loses his girl, the country the war.

The Press

Although the press has a long history in Syria (the first newspapers appeared in Damascus in 1865, Aleppo 1867), it is now another arm of government and party. Historically the Arab press developed most freely and prolifically in Lebanon and Egypt where it was used to propagate ideas of resistance, nationalism and modernization. In Syria there was also considerable activity and for the period of the French Mandate some 90 newspaper titles are listed. Most were very short-lived although one, *al-Baath*, founded by Michel Aflaq, still continues today as the official organ of the party. All newspapers come under the Ministry of Information and are censored, as is news coming from abroad. Other papers appear as government and other party publications, although in content and tone they are basically identical. Journals are published by ministries and other official bodies, for example, sport, agriculture, literature – or more rarely by religious or professional groups. All papers and journals must be licensed by the ministry. Although some critical writing is permitted, newspapers are used as supporters of the government and not as means of investigating scandal or corruption. One newspaper, *al-Thawra* (revolution), established a weekly literary supplement which was published (by Adunis) with considerable freedom to criticize. When requested at least to mention the Baath party, the October war or socialism, the editors refused and the supplement was closed down.

Notes

1 The words of Michel Aflaq in 1955; Baath, *Texts*, p. 135.
2 Halim Barakat, 'Arabic novels and social transformation' in R. Ostle (ed.), *Studies in modern Arabic literature* (Warminster: Aris and Phillips, 1975), pp. 126–7.
3 *Al-mawqif al-adabi*, 76, 1977.
4 Speech by Najah al-Attar, Minister of Culture, *Al-maarifa*, 286, pp. 4–6.
5 Interview with Ikhlasi, *Mulhaq al-uruba al-usbui*, February 1980, p. 9.
6 ibid., p. 10.
7 Miriam Cooke, 'Beirut . . . theatre of the absurd . . . theatre of dreams', *Journal of Arabic Literature*, XIII, p. 128.
8 *Al-maarifa*, 104, 1970, p. 13.
9 ibid., p. 9.
10 He recently felt compelled to leave Beirut for Paris.
11 Quoted from M. M. Badawi, *A critical introduction to modern Arabic poetry* (Cambridge University Press, 1975) p. 234.
12 Salah Dehni in *The cinema in the Arab countries*, ed. G. Sadoul (Beirut: UNESCO, 1966), p. 102.

9 *People and Society*

The age of the masses in the world has come.

(M. Aflaq)

In this chapter the life in a changing environment of the Syrian people, rich and poor, urban and rural, is described. Syria is committed to change brought about by planned development on the basis of a political ideology. While it is possible to describe these changes in political, social or economic terms, it is the individual in his own life, either alone or within a family or larger group, who has to face change and who reacts by adapting and adjusting his personal standards or by clinging more firmly to the familiar and the traditional. A modernizing regime has to deal sensitively with change and with people's feelings, unless it follows the path of totalitarianism and, for example, decrees the abolition of religion or the mass collectivization of all peasant farmers. Yet it is one thing to decide in Damascus to introduce a particular measure, quite another to ensure that peasant or Bedouin in a remote area accepts it.

Islam

Islam has already been referred to in relation to government policy and to the opposition movement which opposes in the name of Islam. The religion of the government, of the Umayyad Mosque and the *ulama* might be called *official* Islam; and at the same time there exists the religion of the hearts and minds of the people, the almost instinctive feelings based on no formal training. Despite rapid modernization and the inflow of Western ideas and technology, Islam still maintains a secure place in Syrian life.

Religion is at its most instinctive among the rural communities. Beliefs tend to be simplistic and perhaps criticized as unorthodox by other Muslims. Different sects may share customs and festivals in villages and rural areas and in the past have had more in common with each other than with their co-religionists in the towns and cities. Lack of education and illiteracy meant that religious knowledge was not in any case very profound. A Christian villager once admitted that 'We are very ignorant. The only difference between our women and those of the Muslims is that they swear by the Prophet and ours by the Virgin.' In addition, certain non-orthodox beliefs are prevalent, beliefs in the power of the evil-eye, of the *jinn* (spirits) whom it is prudent to conciliate, in the efficacy of certain rituals and visits. If the towns are remote, people have felt the need to have a more local and direct contact with religious figures. In this way there developed the cult of local saints. The tomb of a holy man became a place of pilgrimage and the person of the saint a means of obtaining divine blessing and favours. The peasant experienced religion there more at his own level than in the formal atmosphere of the mosque. Prayers and petitions are addressed to the holy man, and women in particular reveal to him their secret wishes, for a husband or a child. Small pieces of cloth are hung as offerings on the tomb. Different saints are renowned for certain characteristics and their abilities to cure. At particular times festivals are held in the vicinity of the tomb and are occasions for celebration and feasting and for the villagers to meet together. A feature of these meetings is the dancing of the *dabka*, a symbol of unity when the dancers (usually divided by sex) interlink in a circle and move round in time to the rhythm of the music.

Another form of gathering is the *sufi* (mystic) service. For centuries in Islamic countries together with the religion of the mosque there has existed that of the mystical orders, groups of men who turned to mysticism as a means of seeking a more direct approach to God. The traditional meetings of these orders is a *dhikr*, a service at which chanting and dancing take place, repeating the name of God and moving around in circles in an effort to achieve a state of mind in which union with God is attained. In some Syrian villages *sufi* meetings take place and villagers attend from the surrounding locality. Governments have been wary of *sufi* organizations, fearing them as alternative centres of loyalty and on occasions as a focus for anti-government feeling. The Baath party is establishing at village level its own organizations which it hopes will replace, or eliminate the need for the more traditional activities. Experience shows, however, that religion in all its forms provides an essential element in people's lives and that education and literacy do not necessarily eliminate the desire for the comfort offered by religion.

A basic feature of Islamic society is the law. In Muslim societies the only law necessary is the *sharia* – the law based on the *Quran* and the traditions of Muhammad and their interpretation. This was sufficient for all relevant aspects of life and society for many centuries. Modern states have had to face legal problems unforeseen by Islamic lawyers and have had to introduce secular laws to complement the Islamic. Civil codes have greatly modified the authority of the *sharia* and law in Syria is now an amalgam of Ottoman, French and Islamic practices. After the first *coup d'état* in 1949 several modifications in legal practice were made. Civil, commercial and criminal codes were promulgated based primarily on French and Islamic legal philosophies. The *waqfs* (religious endowments) were taken out of private hands and transformed into public institutions run by the state. (This was one method of diminishing the authority of the religious leaders.) A secular code has been developed, covering many aspects of personal status, avoiding contradictions with the *sharia* but changing some areas of the status of women and the laws of inheritance. The constitution of 1964 makes it clear, however, that 'Islamic jurisprudence shall be the main source for legislation'. Despite this proviso there are some Sunni Muslims who feel that the secularization of the law has gone too far and the Muslim Brothers demand that all laws contrary to Islam should be abrogated. They believe that one of the essential elements of the unity of Syria is the *sharia* which includes laws adequate to 'organize all aspects of this worldly life and the hereafter at the level of the individual, the family, the nation and the state'.[1]

Class and Society

Syrian society is in a state of transformation. The policies of the Baath and earlier governments have caused changes in the social structure which have had profound implications at all levels.

Traditionally, the class of wealthy landowning and merchant families of Damascus and Aleppo, mostly Sunni Muslims, dominated Syrian political and social life until the Baath takeover. They had had money for several generations made from industrial enterprises and extensive rural landowning. They were usually absentee landlords whose concern was to make money from their land regardless of the conditions of the peasants. In the cities there were members of the old artisan class as well as small merchants and a small working class. The religious teachers (the *ulama*) formed an influential group both as figures in their own right (judges, teachers, officials) and as representatives with the rulers of the urban Sunni masses. They saw their role as the preservation of a stable society in which the practices of Islam could be observed uninterruptedly. They tended to support whichever government was in power in order to maintain their positions of influence. Under a Baathi regime their influence and status have declined.

As in most developing countries there is now in Syria a growing professional and clerical middle class. With the spread of education the numbers of technically and professionally trained men slowly grew during this century, usually men from a modest urban or rural background or the minorities. This new middle class largely stayed outside the patterns of the old loyalties and patronage, gained more influence and looked with suspicion on members of the upper class. The Baathi coup itself had a pronounced class dimension as most of the army officers who ousted the old urban-based leadership were of petty bourgeois or rural origin. They had made their way up into the new class through one of the channels available, the army. These men have, as elsewhere, become the new élite in Syria.

There is still a gap in Syria between town and country, although the traditional relationship between the two is changing. The power of the landlords has been destroyed through land reform and an urban élite no longer dominates the countryside. Small numbers of peasants are moving out of the village into the new middle class and leaving behind their rural life. Half the population is still rural and at the bottom of the scale are the landless peasants. The redistribution of land has brought many of them into the landholding category but 20 per cent remain landless labourers. Their minimum wage and security of employment are low and they have to find work when and where they can. Some seek a new life in the cities where they swell the numbers of the urban poor, finding occupation as street traders, servants, or perhaps as beggars. They hope eventually to find more secure work when, for example, the Euphrates projects begin to need extra labour. At the moment, economically, they remain at the bottom of society.

While not a class as such, the Palestinian refugees form a separate group. They fled from Palestine in 1948, some 100,000 of them, believing that their exile would be temporary and that they would soon return to their family homes and property. Since then, none has returned; nor have they yet been fully integrated into Syrian society. Many live in refugee camps around Damascus and the children attend schools run by the United Nations Relief and Works Agency for Palestinian Refugees, which also funds a vocational training centre in Damascus where places are greatly sought after. The principal of the centre estimated that some two-thirds of his students go on to the Gulf countries to find work. The remainder find jobs in Syria or join the resistance movements. The best students at the centre come from the camps and they use the chance of training to escape from them. The 300,000 Palestinians in Syria (of whom perhaps a third are refugees from later wars in Jordan and Lebanon) enjoy most of the rights of the Syrians, except that they do not have citizenship or a passport – they travel on a temporary document. They are subject to the same laws, do not need permits to obtain work and can join the army or government service. The sense of separateness remains, fuelled by a determination never to abandon the hope that they will one day live in their own country under their own government. Children who have never seen their homeland are taught to believe in their Palestinian identity just as strongly as do their grandparents, the original exiles.

Social Life

In the Middle East the family is at the centre of social life regardless of differences between tribal and settled populations, town and country and classes. In Syria the traditional family structure remains strong. The individual's loyalty is first of all to his family and his standing is determined by his family background, although less now among the more sophisticated circles in the city. Within the extended family, authority rests with the father or grandfather and it looks after its members with a kind of inbuilt social service. Relations are maintained through blood rather than marriage. Responsibility is felt for the honour of the group and particularly for that of its unmarried women. Brothers have murdered sisters who were believed to have lost their virtue. Much affection is shown towards the children and the relationship between mother and son, especially the oldest, is often close. The mother usually becomes known as 'mother of so-and-so' rather than the wife of so-and-so.

Family solidarity is greatly valued and extends to the outside world of government and bureaucracy where family loyalty may outweigh other considerations. It is believed that close or even more distant relatives are the only ones really to be trusted. Things may be done more quickly and easily if there is direct access to relatives. This certainly applies in many private businesses, less so in large nationalized industries. Family ties are guarded as a means of preventing loneliness. Relatives are a means of support against the outside world in times of stress or danger. All members value the home and for women it is the real centre of their lives. Men meet one another outside the home in cafés and clubs. Sometimes family obligations have a negative aspect. Students returning to Syria from Europe complain that it is difficult to work at home because of continual family calls and visits from and to other members. It is almost unheard of to claim to be too busy to see a member of the family.

Children are considered a blessing from God and traditionally the more children (particularly boys) a couple can have the better. They are a sign both of blesssing and of the success of the marriage. Children guarantee that the parents will be looked after in old age and in peasant households that labour is available in the fields. These large families cause the rapid increase in the population which puts a strain on all existing facilities in the country – transport, schooling, housing – and makes the achievement of planning targets more difficult.

Changes in traditional family life are being brought about by education, by migration and emigration into new areas where life has often to be lived without the benefit of family support, and by women's emancipation. The wife in the town has usually led a restricted life, remaining at home to run the household; the peasant wife has run the household and also helped with most agricultural tasks. These roles are being changed by an education which widens the girl's horizons and, increasingly, by the economic necessity for the wife to go out to work herself. The position of women is at the very root of the concept of social change in the Middle East, although there is no consensus about what this position should be. The Baath party was one of the first in the Arab world to demand equality of the sexes and it claimed that 'half of the nation (was) dead and imprisoned behind walls' – that emancipation and equality were necessary to realize its progressive aims. The original Baath constitution asserted that 'the Arab woman enjoys all the rights of citizenship. The party struggles to raise up women's levels in order to make her fit to exercise these rights.'

The 1964 constitution stressed the rights of all citizens without mentioning women specifically. Syrian women are now educated equally, take up employment and enjoy other rights. There is no official move to reverse any of the developments in this area (as, for example, in Iran) and the party is committed to a policy of equality. However, women claim that there is no real equality or emancipation in the minds of the men, that women are regarded as weaker and inferior beings and that much remains to be achieved. The Baath has not tried to intervene in the traditional idea of male guardianship of women. Restraints govern women's social lives and defiance of customs creates general disapproval. The Moral Intelligence Department, part of the security apparatus, investigates every woman seeking government employment. There is a feeling in families that it is still preferable to have sons rather than daughters. One father of seven is reported as saying that he had six daughters and only one child, a son. Very few women go out to work as yet; about 11 per cent of those of working age are economically active, 80 per cent of them in agriculture. They form a quarter of the work force in textiles and one tenth in the tobacco industry. Few work in manufacturing and none in transport. Only 1 per cent of the total hold administrative or managerial posts. In Damascus a small number work in metal or electrical workshops. In the private sector women usually do piece work in their homes.

Syrian women feel discriminated against and this is particularly true in marriage. Within the Muslim community marriages have traditionally been arranged. In the urbanized élite the man and woman have more say over whom they marry and can refuse the family's choice, but with rare exceptions marriage is a family rather than a personal affair. Some young people now rebel against arranged marriages and wish to marry the person of their choice. The Baath party favours marriage although the constitution does not state how it should be arranged. The 1946 version said rather ominously: 'Marriage is a national duty. The state must encourage, facilitate and control it.' This bleak statement was modified slightly in 1964. 'The state shall protect and encourage marriage and shall remove material and social impediments to it.' That these impediments still exist is clear, however, from a study by a Syrian sociologist.[2] He notes a decline in the marriage rate caused by several factors. Voluntary factors – changed morals or attitudes – play little part; the chief causes are housing shortages, inflation, difficulties of meeting the opposite sex, the rising level of education, social and religious gaps and last, but not least, the bride money and the high cost of the wedding. The dowry, according to a religious judge in Damascus, is the main cause of the decline of marriage at a young age – 'a cost added to by all those customs contrary to the spirit of religion – lavish festivities at betrothals and weddings'. The payment of a dowry has become essential in many marriages, a price exacted by the bride's father when a girl's worth is judged in economic terms. Both the government and the religious establishment dislike this state of affairs as they consider it contrary to the interests of society and the *sharia*. But as long as the family is left in control of marriage, and neither the state nor the religious leaders really wants to change this, there is little they can do to discourage the practice. Most young men find it very difficult to raise large sums for the dowry and therefore have to postpone marriage. Equally, young women are intimidated by their families into accepting suitors who can bring large dowries with them. This pressure is strongest in conservative families where there is direct control and oppression. In the more modern families there still seems to be a subtle indoctrination by which girls are brought up to conform to family wishes. In a survey among twenty women students at Damascus University – presumably a liberated milieu – nineteen said they would not consider a romantic relationship with a man without a religious marriage. This attitude was based less on conviction than on their fear of 'laws and customs'. Most also answered that they faced family pressure over marriage.

These attitudes and this kind of pressure are vehemently rejected by Ghada al-Samman who has firmly stated her views on what woman's position in society should be. 'Marriage in my country is, on the whole, a kind of human prostitution, legitimized by two witnesses and a legal document . . . and in its lowering of humankind, marriage is slow death to any kind of individual human creativity or innovativeness.'[3] She is convinced that the position of women in society has to be improved so that the status of marriage is raised. Men must 'correct the individual Arab's mistaken belief that woman, as a species, is inferior and not equal'. Women must be allowed equal rights with men and men must accept this as part of a wider change. She cannot see 'a sexual revolution taking place by itself or existing outside a total revolution of the individual Arab against all that conspires against the realization of his full humanity, all that restricts his freedom and regulates all his relationships'.[4]

Such outspokenness is viewed with horror by the religious

conservatives and by those women who are happy to maintain their traditional roles in subordination to men. In an open letter addressed to Muslim wives in the journal of the Islamic Liberation Front the ideas of the conservatives about the role of women are put very clearly. 'Our community is going through a critical phase. Be a devoted wife helping your husband fulfil his needs . . . The best thing in the world is a devoted woman whose husband regards her as his treasure, whose obedience to him he directs . . . The basis of our faith is obedience, silence and confidence. You represent half the community and its true firm essence if you behave well and bring up your children to be of fine character.'[5] Such sentiments would anger Ghada al-Samman while the conclusion of the letter would probably render her speechless. 'Remember that most of mankind's problems have stemmed from women who have been corrupted and diverted by evil from the truth.'

Syria was the first Arab state to issue legislation on polygamy. The 1953 Law of Personal Status required a Muslim husband to obtain the permission of the courts before he could contract another marriage, which would be given only if he could demonstrate his financial ability to support a second wife. Divorce was traditionally very simple for the man. He merely had to say aloud three times 'I divorce you' to his wife (in her presence or not) and a divorce was legalized. Now in Syria, court permission is required before a man may repudiate his wife. The manifesto of the Islamic revolution does not specifically mention divorce although it seeks equality of rights for all citizens providing the rights of the woman do not affect her duty towards her home, husband and children. The man's duty is to protect and provide for his family. It is not clear, therefore, how divorce would be regulated under an Islamic government.

A sensitive area of family life is the question of contraception. It is the answer to the problem of a rapidly growing population and of overcrowding, but there is considerable reluctance to be overcome and the government has not yet sponsored an official family-planning programme. Religious opposition has not been notable and there is no absolute prohibition in Islamic law. There is more concern among husbands and mothers-in-law who consider large families proof of potency and a happy marriage. There is also a marked ignorance of birth control methods especially among illiterate women. In 1973 the Syrian government organized a questionnaire for a number of married women aged 15–45 on family size and contraception. They were selected from all classes from town and country. 60 per cent were illiterate. Many of these women faced a life of continual pregnancy and accepted this as their lot. Most knew nothing of contraception while others could envisage the idea of family planning without necessarily putting it into practice. Half the sample agreed with its usage as a means of keeping families small, of preserving the health of the mother, and for financial reasons. Women who knew of contraception and did not practise it gave as reasons, husband's opposition, health risks of the pill and religious prohibition. Older women accepted the situation of continuous childbirth while the younger, more educated ones wanted to limit their families to two or three children.

Village Life

Peasants comprise about half the population of Syria. They live in villages scattered throughout the country following a way of life that has developed over the centuries. They live in Druze mountain villages, in communities on the edge of the desert and in villages by the sea. They lead a life bound to the climate and the soil that has only slowly opened itself to the outside world. Radio and television now depict new horizons; education and migration alter traditional patterns of behaviour and thought, and the party has made strenuous efforts to integrate the peasant into the new way of life it is establishing in Syria. It is, nevertheless, the most traditional of societies and probably the most difficult to change. The peasant does not adopt change for its own sake. He has to be convinced of its benefit to himself and his family, particularly in the economic sphere. Peasants have a healthy scepticism of changes emanating from the city or government, but once convinced they are often enthusiastic supporters.

The urban landlords who dominated the countryside used their land as a source of wealth and power. The peasants had no say in this system and needed the protection of a powerful landlord or patron if they wanted their rights to be respected at all. The peasants naturally remained on the fringe of the political system, uninvolved and powerless. The government was remote and powerful, to be submitted to if unavoidable, to be evaded if possible. Most peasants remained indifferent to the politics of Damascus and were much more concerned with local solidarity or conflict. Villages offered a façade of solidarity to the outside world while within they were often split with rivalry and feuds. This state was summed up in the folk saying: 'My brother and I against my cousin; my cousin and I against the outsider.' The family held peasant life together and the individual was virtually unknown outside his family. This compensated for the lack of state concern or for a greater loyalty to the homeland. The family provided the refuge against the outside world.

Economically the peasants were not well off and were to a large extent exploited by absentee landlords, by moneylenders and merchants. The majority of peasants were share-croppers. The land was controlled from outside and the prices they received for their crops were also out of their control. As they were unable to take their produce to market, or to wait for better prices, they had to accept the prices offered locally. They often wrested a bare living from the soil, working for the benefit of others. As peasants say cynically: 'He who owns does not work and he who works does not own.' Even when peasants owned their land the plots were often not viable. They were too small or in undesirable areas. The peasants were unable to make any profits and depended on urban merchants to provide for their needs at high prices and they became debtors from whom the merchants took their surplus when prices were at their lowest.

The share-croppers had even less security. They worked for large owners and could retain as little as 16 per cent of their crops. In addition, peasants often had to give personal service to the landlord, labour or their daughters for domestic help. At the bottom of the scale were the landless labourers who moved around in search of work. At harvest time they could retain a twelfth to a sixteenth of their work. Education passed them by as there were few village schools and they were unable to move out of their surroundings or up the social scale.

From its earliest constitution the Baath party was socialist and dedicated to a just redistribution of wealth. Ownership of land was to be limited so that the owner himself could exploit it without exploiting others. Peasant unions were promised in order to protect peasant rights, raise living standards and bring their members more directly into the life of the nation. When the Baath took power they began to put some of their policies into practice. They were dedicated to creating more opportunities and equality for the peasants and to improving the general economic situation of the country by reforming agricultural production. They also undertook to extend their control throughout the country among the peasant communities by setting up a countrywide organization which stretches from the government in the centre down to district and village levels. As far as possible there are cells and branches in each village which act as bases of local leadership replacing the traditional structure which largely disappeared when land was redistributed and the holdings of large landlords broken up. The local branches work to mobilize the peasants and to ensure that party policy is known and carried out at the lowest level. Once a peasant has joined the party he is eligible for membership of its bodies which advise on policy and he may be elected to attend party congresses. He can thus hope to make his voice heard at the centre of power.

A Peasant Bureau oversees rural policy at the highest level and co-ordinates the activities of other bodies established to develop agriculture, peasant unions, agricultural and co-operative banks, marketing offices. All these bodies together with the co-operatives themselves have been set up in order to remedy the past state of affairs – the banks to eliminate the necessity of money lenders, the co-operatives to improve methods of productivity, the marketing boards to ensure fair prices. The General Federation of Peasants is the main organization for peasant interests. It has trained a group of activists of small and middle peasants who work their own land to spread the party message among their fellow workers. They attend peasant union schools where party ideology is taught and where the teachers try to awaken a sense of national political awareness.

Great changes have been wrought in the life of the peasant and they are now more integrated into the nation, are better off and appreciate government efforts to improve their conditions. There remain many problems. Some peasants join the party for personal ambition rather than with the desire to help their colleagues; local notables try to retain their influence; there is a lack of trained experts, and peasants may offer servile flattery to officials while still clinging to their own traditions. The peasant, naturally conservative and wary, may also treat government policy with a great deal of scepticism. The scene in Maghut's *Hunchback sparrow* humorously illustrates this attitude. In a village the peasants are awaiting a visit from the Agricultural Commissioner who is not really expected to arrive. He does eventually show up – briefly: 'What has he done then?' 'Nothing. Nothing. He stuck his head out of the window of his car at the first field he came to, glanced at it as though at his watch, and then turned homewards with a yawn.'

The case of one peasant vividly illustrates how change has affected rural life and how tradition and change may have to be lived with together. The example comes from a study made by a sociologist of four Syrian villages.[6] In a village near Damascus the local party head is the third son of a medium peasant who was sent by his family to university while the older sons remained at home to look after the land. He was selected to be their link with the *new* outside world. He joined the party at school and after the Baath gained power was given the task of organizing youth activities. By village standards he was doing well and on the way up. His case is the common one in Syria of a peasant making his way through education and politics. He is *modern* in this sense and in his leadership he has replaced the authority of the traditional village elders. In other respects his behaviour remains traditional. His wife is veiled and in seclusion and his friends, who are more liberal, do not see her. He says that he does this in order to retain the respect of the more conservative villagers. In his private life he remains traditional while he deals in public with women in their federation and youth union. In the village itself the party is quite active and the younger men have assumed the political roles. They represent the young Baath against the traditional village elders. They have succeeded in forming two co-operatives among the peasants who tend now to look upon the party chief as the person who can help them to solve their problems through his access to officials in Damascus.

Although this example is of one village only, it can be taken to show how the peasant's life is gradually changing and of how the Baath is spreading its influence.

The Bedouin

The Baath is very clear in its attitude towards the Bedouin population of Syria. Its constitution states that: 'Nomadism is a primitive state . . . The party struggles for the sedentarization of nomads by grants of land to them, for the abolition of tribal customs, and for the application to them of the law of the state.' The constitution was of course drawn up by city dwellers. In fact, nomadism is a highly organized way of life, making full use of scarce water and other supplies, of the abilities of the camel and the availability of pasturing. Governments dislike the Bedouin because they are not settled and therefore difficult to control, and because they have a tendency to ignore international frontiers. They have also been unruly marauders who encroached on their settled neighbours. Bedouin form some 7 per cent of the population, and this proportion is gradually decreasing through settlement, the use of motor transport and the application of state laws. They belong to eight nomadic tribes living in the arid and semi-arid areas of Syria. They are herders and 35,000 families look after some three-fifths of the total sheep population which they take on annual migration into the desert after the winter rainy season. When the vegetation dries up the sheep return to eat stubble and weeds on the edge of the cultivated areas. In dry seasons the flocks suffer and migration is difficult. The Bedouin who depend on sheep and goats are among the poorest section of the population. Traditionally they regulate their own affairs with a shaykh at the head of each tribe and disputes are settled by him (or the heads of sub-groups) according to customary law. Women play a full part in Bedouin life. They and the young girls care for the young or sick animals, milk the goats, sheep and camels, and set up and dismantle the camps when the household moves on its migrations. The men and boys herd the animals and use the camels as beasts of burden.

An interesting change has come about in Bedouin life. Now outside many tents instead of camels grazing a small truck is parked. This gives the Bedouin much greater mobility and earning power. The men say that a motor vehicle is much more reliable than a camel, which tends to wander away and finds walking on paved roads difficult and hazardous. They can now migrate more quickly and one truck can do the work of several men and camels. The women on the other hand complain that the camel used to be the centre of their lives – milking was done collectively, as was rug-making from camel wool, and they generally felt an emotional attachment to their animals. The truck has taken away a part of their communal life and enjoyment. It is also true that to the outsider a Toyota pickup can never have the romantic appeal of the Bedouin camel.

Town and City

In 1960 the urban population of Syria comprised 30 per cent of the total, in 1970 46 per cent and is at present about half. This growth in city dwelling has been spread throughout Syrian towns but has been particularly high in Damascus and to a lesser extent in Aleppo. These developments place a great strain on the facilities of the towns and pose very severe problems for development. Syria is fortunate, however, in having several urban centres which attract migrants and not all the growth is concentrated in one place. Although Damascus is the centre of government, Aleppo remains a very important regional centre. Smaller towns are growing for particular reasons, Tabqa because of the dam, Latakia as a port, Homs and Tartus as centres of oil refining. Damascus and Aleppo contain the largest numbers of industrial workers and all industries are to be found in the two cities.

Since 1973 the growth of Damascus has been considerable. It has spread into neighbouring areas, swallowing agricultural and orchard lands where new suburbs and satellite towns have been built. The increased areas of settlement cause problems of traffic congestion, of water supplies and pollution. The housing shortage is severe despite the large amount of building that has taken place, mainly new flats in new areas. The older houses are cheaper to rent but they bring in little income and are often overcrowded. The shortage makes marriage difficult for couples who find it financially impossible to move into the new apartments. In 1970 it was estimated that more than 25,000 housing units were needed and this number has since increased. Some of the older quarters have been demolished as they become dilapidated to make way for new roads and junctions. Shanty and poorly built instant-homes for rural immigrants have developed more or less haphazardly outside the city and, although they may have electricity they are often without running water or sewerage.

The migrant into the city has to cross the gulf between town and country and has to adjust to a new atmosphere and way of life. This causes problems, particularly to the female members of the family. The link with village solidarity has been broken and there are no longer the same opportunities to meet friends in the street or round the village water supply. If possible, relatives or migrants from one village try to live near to each other and offer help in finding accommodation and jobs. Among the young men two types migrate, the have-nots and the bright ones in search of education and opportunities. The former have to make do with what they can find in the way of employment, sharing rooms with other migrants and scratching a living. Some have to resort to begging and in 1986 a 1974 law against begging was reactivated in an effort to combat organized rings of beggars operating in middle-class areas in Damascus and other towns. Beggars were to be rounded up and the social services would decide who were in genuine need. The old and disabled would be housed in 'homes of dignity' and the young taken to training centres.

In Europe migration to cities usually occurred together with industrialization. In a developing country industry does not yet offer the same opportunities. In any case as industry becomes more technological the demand is growing for technicians with the highest skills and unskilled labourers can often find only the most menial jobs. Factory conditions are much better in the public sector and workers in the private are sometimes exploited and receive wages below the legal minimum. If wages are too low many workers are forced to take on second jobs. After factory work, a worker may spend the rest of the day as an itinerant salesman, an artisan or a waiter in a café. Workers in the private sector rarely have the same services as the state provides, such as transport, cafeterias and medical care.

It is sometimes difficult for the new worker to adapt to factory life. Managers complain of absenteeism and a high turnover. The rural immigrant has to accept new conditions changing from working with the seasons and daylight to working to an often monotonous time schedule. The experience of one woman migrant illustrates this change. She reported: 'I used to live in the village, far from the city but with the water shortage peasants began to migrate toward the city in search of work. People said you could have everything there – salaries, bonuses, benefits and services. Thanks to factory work . . . we all went [to the city] . . . We lived among villagers like ourselves with the same customs and traditions. Everyone worked in the local factories . . .' When she married and had a baby she still continued to work. 'After my maternity leave my sister-in-law took care of my baby so I could keep my job. I left him with her at 6 o'clock in the morning and I was allowed to leave work at 2.0 p.m. because I was nursing, but I never got home before 3.15 p.m. because of the transportation problem.'[7]

Notes

1 U. F. Abd-Allah, *The Islamic struggle in Syria* (Berkeley: Mizan, 1983), p. 234.

2   Bu Ali Yasin, *Dirasat arabiya*, August, 1978.
3   Ghada Samman, in *Mawaqif* 2, no. 12, pp. 68–72.
4   ibid.
5   *Al-nazeer*, no. 83, pp. 15, 16.
6   Condensed from R. Hinnebusch, *Party and peasant in Syria* (Cairo Papers in Social Sciences, 1, 1979), p. 76.
7   Quoted in MERIP (Middle East Research and Information Project) Reports, July/August 1985, p. 23.

10   Conclusion

> The Arab future will only be realized as we wish it
> through Arab unity and the feeling that we are a
> great nation.   (M. Aflaq)

Syria used to be known for its military coups and instability. Since
1964 one party has been in power and since 1970 one man, Hafiz
al-Asad. How has he retained power? He is not a man in the mould
of Jamal Abd al-Nasser who retained power largely through
personal charisma. Asad is a skilled politician who has tried to
develop both a personal following and a state and party apparatus
which legitimizes his and his government's position and gives the
people a permanent interest in the regime. In addition he has built
up the army as the main prop of the state. If these structures are
durable and cohesive then the regime should survive his passing.
The people develop a stake in the status quo and rely on the state for
education, employment and advancement. Asad has also been a
pragmatic, usually cautious leader who consults his supporters and
keeps them in positions of influence. While carefully strenghtening
ties with fellow Alawis he has tried not to alienate the Sunni
majority. All stirrings of opposition have been ruthlessly dealt with.
   Syria often has had a bad press in the outside world, most recently
standing accused of participation in terrorist activity. What is the
reason for this reputation? The Syrians are single-mindedly devoted
to certain aims and the apparent determination not to compromise
makes them difficult to deal with. As a leader of Arab nationalism,
Syria has to pursue a relentlessly uncompromising anti-Israeli
policy in the effort at the very least to regain Jaulan and ultimately
to settle the Palestinian problem. Many methods are adopted to try
to achieve these ends and to demonstrate that no settlement in the
Middle East is possible without Syrian participation. Arab states
who are thought to weaken in their resolve to oppose Israel are
condemned as traitors to the Arab cause. There is something rather
remarkable in this unwavering determination. Asad has described it
thus:

Our nation needs to adhere to principles, the relinquishing of which, as we know, leads to a kind of surrender, which others desire to impose on our nation. We shall not be deceived by ambiguous titles and names; we must be concerned with the essence of things and call them by their right names . . . This understanding, this view, is our point of departure. Therefore, I say that they will not succeed in luring us into positions of surrender; they will never succeed in tempting us into accepting what we do not want. Peace is the peace that you make and surrender is the surrender you reject.[1]

This policy inevitably imposes a huge burden on Syria. Facing Israel necessitates the maintenance of strong armed forces which will deter direct confrontation. Syria is seeking an honourable settlement in the area. This will have to mean eventual compromise and at the moment there is little sign of this. And Syria's self-imposed role as policeman in Lebanon is an additional drain on scarce resources. Withdrawal can come about only when Israel also withdraws and when the Lebanese themselves agree on their own future.

Asad's long-term ambitions for Syria are very clearly outlined in the 250 pages of the latest five-year plan. The economic, social and educational development of the country is an ambition difficult to achieve even if there were no political, military or manpower restraints. All policies are necessarily compromises and as long as Syria faces these restraints internal development will be slowed. Syria will continue to try to achieve progress on all fronts, struggling to overcome external threats, and fighting, in Asad's words, to realize 'the objectives of the Arab nation – unity, liberty and socialism'.

Note

1   Speech, February 1982, *Journal of Palestine Studies*, XII, 3, p. 239.

Chronology of Events

1918	October	Faisal enters Damascus.
1920	April	Mandate system established.
	July	French defeat Syrians and occupy the country.
1925–7		Druze revolt.
1928		First elections to Syrian Assembly.
		Hashim al-Atasi, President.
1936	September	Franco-Syrian treaty signed.
1939		Alexandretta ceded to Turkey.
1941	June	British and Free French forces oust Vichy French.
1943		Movement of Aflaq and Bitar takes name of Baath.
1946	April	French finally withdraw.
1947	July	Elections; Quwatli President.
1948–9		War in Palestine.
1949	March	Coup of Husni al-Zaim.
	August	Coup of Sami Hinnawi.
	December	Coup of Adib al-Shishakli.
1950	February	Foundation of Arab Socialist Party.
1951	December	Shishakli takes power for the army.
1952	April	Political parties suspended and opposition press banned.
1954	February	Shishakli resigns.
	September	Elections; Baath gains seats.
1955	October	Military pact with Egypt.
1956	February	Soviet arms supplied.
	October	Tripartite attack on Suez.
1958	February	Creation of United Arab Republic.
1961	September	Coup to take Syria out of the UAR.
	December	Elections; Baath successful.
1963	March	Baath–army coup.
	May	First Baath government under Amin al-Hafiz.
1966	February	Coup led by Salah Jadid.
1967	June	Six-day war against Israel; Jaulan occupied.
1969	February	Struggle between Jadid and Hafiz al-Asad.
1970	September	Aborted Syrian intervention in Jordan to help Palestinians.
	November	Asad seizes power.
1971	March	Asad elected President.
1972	March	National Progressive Front dominated by Baath established.

1973	October	War against Israel.
1976	June	Syrian troops enter Lebanon.
1977	November	Sadat visits Jerusalem.
1978	February	Asad re-elected President.
1979	June	Cadets killed in Aleppo.
1980	July	Bitar assassinated in Paris.
1981	December	Jaulan annexed by Israel.
1982	February	Revolt in Hama.
	June	Israeli invasion of Lebanon.
1983	November	Syrians fight PLO in Tripoli.
1985	February	Asad re-elected President.
1986	October	Diplomatic relations between Britain and Syria suspended.

Important Personalities

AFLAQ, Michel	Founder of Baath Party 1943; secretary-general of the party; resigned 1965.
ASAD, Hafiz	Colonel; member of Baath Military Committee 1966; State President 1971–
ASAD, Rifaat	Brother of Hafiz; Vice-President.
ATASI, Hashim	Prime Minister in Faisal's government; President of the Assembly 1928; State President 1936.
ATASI, Nur al-Din	State President 1966.
BAKDASH, Khalid	Leader of Syrian Communist Party; first Communist member of an Arab parliament.
BITAR, Salah al-Din	Co-founder of Baath Party 1943; Foreign Minister 1956; Prime Minister 1963; assassinated 1980.
HAFIZ, Amin	Brigadier; Minister of Interior 1963; President of National Revolutionary Council 1964; ousted 1966.
HAWRANI, Akram	Founder of Arab Socialist Party; united with Baath 1952.
JABIRI, Saadallah	Minister of Interior 1936.
JADID, Salah	Member of Baath Military Committee 1966; ousted 1970.
KHURI, Faris	Served in Faisal's government; founder of People's Party 1925; Speaker of Assembly 1936; President of Assembly 1947; Prime Minister 1954.
MARDAM, Jamil	Prime Minister 1936, 1947.
QUWATLI, Shukri	Minister of Finance 1936; State President 1943, 1947.
SAADA, Antun	Founder of Syrian National Party.
SARRAJ, Abdel Hamid	Chief of Intelligence, Minister of Interior in UAR.
SHAHBANDAR, Abd al-Rahman	Served in Faisal's government; founder of People's Party 1925.
SHISHAKLI, Adib	Colonel, led coup of 1949; resigned 1954.
TLAS, Mustafa	Chief of Staff 1970; Minister of Defence.
ZAIM, Husni	Colonel, led coup of 1948.

Bibliography

This list includes the books found most useful in writing this study. Not all the items are of equal value but the interested reader may use them as a guide to further study.

Fuller bibliographies

Hourani, A. H. 'Syria and Lebanon' in the Middle East Libraries Committee's *Middle East and Islam; a bibliographical introduction*, ed. by D. Grimwood-Jones (Zug, 1979).

Seccombe, I. J. *Syria* (Oxford: Clio Press, 1987).

Sluglett, P. and Farouk-Sluglett, M. 'Syria and Lebanon' in the Middle East Libraries Committee's *Middle East and Islam; a bibliographical introduction. Supplement 1977–1983*, ed. by P. Auchterlonie (Zug, 1986).

History

Hourani, A. H. *Syria and Lebanon: a political essay* (Oxford: Chatham House, 1946). A succinct appreciation.

Khoury, P. S. *Urban notables and Arab nationalism; the politics of Damascus, 1860–1920* (Cambridge: Cambridge University Press, 1983).

Khoury, P. S. *Syria and the French Mandate; the politics of Arab nationalism 1920–45* (London: I. B. Tauris, 1987).

Petran, T. *Syria* (London: Ernest Benn, 1972). A very good survey.

Seale, P. *The struggle for Syria: a study of post-war Arab politics 1945–1958* (London: I. B. Tauris, repr. 1986). The best study of the period.

Modern Politics and History

Abd-Allah, U. F. *The Islamic struggle in Syria* (Berkeley: Mizan Press, 1983).

Aflaq, M. *Choice of texts from the Ba'th party founder's thought* (Florence, 1977).

Devlin, J. F.   *The Ba'th Party: a history from its origins to 1966* (Stanford: Hoover Institution Press, 1976).

Devlin, J. F.   *Syria; modern state in an ancient land* (Boulder: Westview Press, 1983). Very good introduction.

Hinnebusch, R.   *Party and peasant in Syria; rural politics and social change under the Ba'th* (Cairo Papers in Social Sciences, 3, 1; Cairo: American University, 1979).

Kerr, M.   *The Arab cold war; Gamal 'Abd al-Nasir and his rivals, 1958–1970* (London: Oxford University Press for Chatham House, 3rd edn, 1971). A study of Iraqi-Syrian-Egyptian negotiations and interesting for its verbatim quotations.

Ma'oz, M. (ed.).   *Syria under Assad* (London: Croom Helm, 1986). Useful articles on politics and economics.

Nyrop, R. F. (ed.)   *Syria; a country study* (Washington, DC: American University, 3rd edn, 1979). Comprehensive survey.

Olson, R. W.   *The Ba'th and Syria 1947 to 1982; the evolution of ideology, party and state* (Princeton: Kingston Press, 1982).

Raymond, A. (ed.).   *La Syrie d'aujourd'hui* (Paris: Centre d'Etudes et de Recherches sur l'Orient Arabe Contemporain, 1980). Articles by leading French scholars.

Van Dam, N.   *The struggle for power in Syria; sectarianism, regionalism and tribalism in politics* (London: Croom Helm, 2nd edn, 1981). The best on its subject.

Economy

International Bank for Reconstruction and Development   *The economic development of Syria* (Baltimore: Johns Hopkins University, 1955).

Kanovsky, E.   *The economic development of Syria* (Tel Aviv: University Publishing, 1977).

See also Ma'oz and Raymond above. The *Middle East Economic Digest* has regular up-to-date reports.

Literature

Several English translations of literary works by Syrian authors have now been published. They are scattered through various anthologies. M. M. Badawi lists most of them in his two bibliographies, 'Modern Arabic Literature' in the bibliographical introduction and supplement referred to above.

Index